WELCOME TO THE FUNNEL

Proven Tactics to Turn Your Social Media and Content Marketing Up to 11

JASON A MILLER

Rock n Roll ~

Jason Miller

Cover design by Scorch

Editing by Ten Ton Marketing

Illustrations—Fiverr

TABLE OF CONTENTS

SIDE 2: SOCIAL

SIDE 3: ALL TOGETHER NOW

SIDE 4: APPENDIX AND SPECIAL THANKS

Praise for Welcome to the Funnel

"Storytelling, rock n roll, and secrets to creating remarkable content. B2B marketing just got sexier. Pay attention, marketers! A must-have guide to creating content that rocks is here."

–Ekaterina Walter, *Author of the Wall Street Journal bestseller "Think Like Zuck" and co-author of "The Power of Visual Storytelling"*

"This book is a little like having Axl Rose show up in your living room to play a house party. You can't help but be blown away."

–Ann Handley, *Chief Content Officer at MarketingProfs, Wall Street Journal bestselling author of Everybody Writes: Your Go-To Guide to Creating Ridiculously Good Content*

"To stand out in the jungle of information available online, you need content marketing that truly rocks. Jason Miller just supplied the playbook: a step-by-step guide for filling the all-important top of the funnel. A must read!"

–Jay Baer, *New York Times best-selling author of Youtility*

"Jason Miller is to content marketing what guitarist Vivian Campbell is to metal. He's rocked with everyone in the business, and he's played on countless hits. In "Welcome to the Funnel," Miller brings an ensemble band together to provide a boxed set of rocking content licks."

–Joe Chernov, *VP of Marketing (Content), HubSpot*

"Jason Miller isn't going to waste your time with theory or pontification. This book is jammed full of immediately useful best practices, marketing hacks and other practical tips to accelerate the impact, efficiency and ROI of your marketing efforts. Time to turn it up to eleven!"

–Matt Heinz, *President, Heinz Marketing Inc*

"Jason is a content marketing rockstar! It isn't because of the great content virtually every marketer has seen since he has been at Marketo and LinkedIn (and he had the metrics to prove it), but because of how he breaks down every detail needed to have an amazing content "road show." Jason shares how to get your content produced, how to make it stand out from the noise, how to make sure it is getting shared and how to measure its success. If you are looking to amplify your content marketing success, your team must read this book."

–Bryan Eisenberg, *New York Times best-selling author of Waiting for Your Cat to Bark and Buyer Legends*

"B2B marketing has been boring for far too long. Jason's love of rock n roll infused with his experience makes for an interesting read, and even more interesting applications."

–Michael Brenner, *Marketing Blogger, Speaker and Head of Strategy, NewsCred*

"This is the type of book I like to read with real anecdotes and examples mixed with specific step-by-step guidance. And almost as importantly, the book is truly entertaining. If you are trying to understand content marketing, social media, and modern demand generation, then this is your book. You can read it in a day and it will change your game."

–Craig Rosenberg, *Chief Analyst, TOPO and Editor, Funnelholic.com*

ABOUT THE AUTHOR

Jason Miller leads global content and social initiatives for LinkedIn Marketing Solutions, helping marketers understand how to use LinkedIn to achieve their marketing goals and deliver real ROI. Previously he was the senior manager of social media strategy at Marketo and responsible for leading the company's content and social media efforts. Before entering the B2B space, he spent ten years at Sony developing and executing marketing campaigns around the biggest names in music.

When he is not building campaigns, creating remarkable content, and tracking the ROI of social, he is winning awards as a concert photographer, singing 80's metal karaoke, and winning at Seinfeld trivia. Jason is a frequent contributor to Content Marketing Institute, Social Media Examiner, MarketingProfs, and Copyblogger, and has presented at numerous industry conferences including Dreamforce, Social Media Marketing World, Social Fresh, Inbound, Content Marketing World, Microsoft Convergence, and more.

To my beautiful wife Tricia;
without her none of this would have been possible.

FOREWORD

Too many business books feel like cover bands. They might be entertaining enough, but ultimately what they deliver feels a little lacking—a substitute for the real deal.

Which is why I love this new book from Jason Miller—the one that you're now about to read—and that's why I'm here telling you why you will be glad you picked it up.

This isn't a book that comes close to the mark but ultimately leaves you feeling unsatisfied. This isn't a book of inexplicit generalities and amorphous marketing platitudes.

Instead, this book delivers the how-to know-how you need to create content that will deliver results for your organization. It's a detailed guide that will, as Jason says, turn your own content marketing up to an 11.

Why am I confident of that?

Because Jason Miller is the real deal.

He's not co-opting someone else's playlist to tell you what works and why; instead, he's created his own. By experimenting, innovating, and iterating—and with his own blood, sweat, and tears (see what I did there?)—he has homed in on what works.

And now he's generously sharing his playlist with you.

This book is a little like having Axl Rose show up in your living room to play a house party. You can't help but be blown away.

— **Ann Handley**, Chief Content Officer at MarketingProfs
Wall Street Journal bestselling author of *Everybody Writes: Your Go-To Guide to Creating Ridiculously Good Content* (Wiley 2014) Boston, MA

INTRODUCTION

It was a Tuesday in the summer of 2009 that I decided to leave an industry I loved. It was the only job I had had since graduating college. 12 years in the music industry began back in 1997 when record sales were at an all-time high. This celebration would be short-lived with the introduction of the MP3, a day that every one of my former colleagues remembers well.

Fast forward a decade or so and the industry that was thrilled to be charging $18.99 for a compact disc (which many times customers were buying for only one song) was crumbling from within. It was a depressing time to be in the music biz, and every day the news just got more and more bleak. The day I decided to do something about it was just another new-release Tuesday. (The day that new music was released each and every week.) The number-one selling record on the Billboard chart was the new record from Cake. I love that band and was thrilled for their #1 debut; the only problem was that it had only sold 47,000 copies that week. This was the lowest debut ever in the history of Billboard. That was the last nail in the coffin for me.

I decided it was time to go back to school. I started by taking a few classes and pursuing my master's degree in business, but when I found out that it would take 3-4 years, that option went out the window. I found a digital marketing program offered by UC Berkeley and dove in headfirst. I was working full time and taking two or three classes a week learning SEM, SEO, email marketing, social media, you name it —anything and everything I could to sharpen my skill set.

After about a year of no sleep and burning the candle at both ends, I was ready to make a move. I applied for probably around 40 or so jobs with not one single reply. My future wife to be, a seasoned tech marketer, would come into my life and play a pivotal role. At that time

I was writing for a physical newspaper and she suggested that I start a blog; I remember asking her, "How do you do that?" I was convinced that she was from the future or something. She would later introduce me to a friend of hers who worked at a small company that needed a social media manager. I remember sending that person an email saying that I was a social media expert, when in fact I was still a novice (and who the hell says that in the first place, right? I know better now). Somehow I got an interview and the fact that I had a personal blog on Blogger, a hundred or so Twitter followers, and a very enthusiastic attitude was enough for them to take a chance on me.

If that moment never happened, I would not be where I am today. The fact that I had the digital classes under my belt, figured out how to Tweet pretty well, and wrote a very basic free blog was enough to get me in the door and I was grateful. From there I began to hustle. This meant chasing down thought leaders, buying and reading their books, going to every single conference I possibly could and asking countless times to guest blog for them. My first break was when Ann Handley[1] happened to read some of the content I was posting and said I should do a guest blog for the MarketingProfs Daily Fix[2]. I submitted a post to her the next day.

Then it was Social Media Today[3], Social Media Examiner[4], 60 Second Marketer, etc. These were the blogs that I loved to read (and still do) and I simply reached out (not really simply; it took quite a while to convince these folks that I had the blogging chops). But it finally happened. I'm not sure if they actually liked my ideas or were just tired of the countless emails I sent asking if I could contribute. The bottom line here is that I did a tremendous amount of blogging and writing for free. Meaning, I didn't get paid. But the value of the exposure and sharing my ideas outside of my personal blog paid off. I did this for about a year and a half non-stop. It was an experiment in getting better at writing, while building a personal brand.

That was around the time that I started working at Marketo, the leader in marketing automation applications. It's also when I doubled down on my efforts. Marketo was still a startup at that time and it was moving fast. I remember my interview was focused on how well I balance strategy and execution. I would quickly learn that there is indeed a delicate balance between the two and it's important to find and maintain that balance. I learned more in two years at Marketo than I did in my entire career; it was like getting a Master's Degree in modern marketing at an accelerated pace. There are no shortage of ideas and books on what to do, but measurement and answering "How do you know it's working?" is bleeding edge and the folks at Marketo are leading the way.

Then LinkedIn called. I was not even looking for a change, but when they told me about their content initiatives, I was hooked. The opportunity to be part of a content movement of this magnitude was too great to pass up. The beauty of this move is that I would again be marketing to marketers so my strategy and tactics could easily be applied but under my own direction this time around. By the way, I have heard marketers say that I have it easier than they do because I get to "market to marketers." While that may be the case in some instances, the fact that you are putting your campaigns in front of other marketers opens yourself up to be measured by your peers, and judged by the very marketer with whom you wish to connect. In that case, I would say that it's much harder because marketers know other marketers' tactics and can see through the bulls**t.

On July 15, 2014 I celebrated my one-year anniversary at LinkedIn along with my birthday. I have learned a ton here and to be honest, I've never been happier in my career. I haven't slowed down one bit and I still do my very best to write as many guest blogs as I possibly can, and respond to every single request I get for content/tips/interviews, etc. It never gets easier but the fact that I have met so many amazing people throughout this transition keeps me wanting to do more.

Oh, I almost forgot to mention… The music industry will always be a part of my life. I keep that part of my past alive and well with my concert photography and music blogging[5]. My passion will always be rock 'n' roll and heavy metal. There is almost always some element of KISS, Judas Priest, or Guns N' Roses in my content and sometimes I even use my own rock 'n' roll photography and anecdotes to "enhance" my presentations. If you can inject your personality into what you do and the message you share, you'll be one step ahead in the content marketing game.

Audiences can sense when a person is passionate about a certain topic and whether or not they are sincere in their message and delivery. In addition, passion adds credibility and trust, which I find missing in much of the content on the web today. It may not translate to every individual, but then again you can't please everyone, and you certainly shouldn't be trying to in the first place. I wear my rock 'n' roll heart on my sleeve and never pretend to be someone I'm not. That's the most important lesson I've learned through all of this and my best advice to anyone interested in traveling a similar road.

What's next? This book. Everything I have learned over the past 4-5 years pulled together with my passion for rock 'n' roll.

1. http://www.annhandley.com/
2. http://www.marketingprofs.com/opinions/
3. http://www.socialmediaexaminer.com/
4. http://60secondmarketer.com/blog/
5. http://rocknrollcocktail.com/

CHAPTER 1

Death of the One-Dimensional Marketer

When I first entered the B2B marketing space in 2009, I experienced a bit of marketing culture shock. Up until that point, I had worked in the B2C space, and because the B2B world was so different, I literally had to go back to school to hone my digital marketing chops.

My learning curve aside, a shift was taking place in the B2B marketing industry at that time: social media was just starting to take off, and no one was doing B2B social marketing well. We marketers simply didn't have the experience. So, measuring the ROI of social media marketing was completely out of the question. The best we could hope for was to make some sort of un-quantifiable—but positive—impact on our overall marketing by engaging in untested social media marketing tactics.

What I discovered during this time would become a crucial part of a marketing philosophy that has served me well in my career: *Being a one-dimensional marketer is simply not a good way to get ahead in the B2B world.*

Today's successful marketers aren't just good at one thing; we are *hybrid marketers.* We don't specialize in social media, email marketing or direct mail. Instead, we integrate all the old and new marketing channels into one overall marketing strategy. We are, you might say, Renaissance Marketers.

Rise of the Renaissance Marketers: Masters of Social, Content, Email, SEO, and Analytics

As hybrid marketers, we aren't just dabblers; we are practitioners. We go out of our way to master the tactics and strategies that make up a completely integrated marketing approach. We are willing to learn new things and constantly change our skill set and points of view to serve our end goals.

To that end, we hybrid marketers must stay on top of five areas of strategy in the ever-changing, highly competitive marketing landscape:

Social—The first and most important step to succeeding with social marketing is to be personally active on social media. Show me a marketing exec with a successful corporate program, and I'll show you an exec who writes his own Tweets. In order to truly understand how social channels can be used for sales and marketing, marketers have to be both active and proficient. It's this type of hands-on engagement that helps marketers identify opportunities. For example, seeing a hot topic being discussed in the social sphere can be the catalyst for a new content asset.

Keeping a finger on the pulse in this way means no shortcuts, and no hiring a proxy. But you *can* enlist the help of your entire organization.

As Bryan Eisenberg wrote in a blog post entitled The Shake Weight Challenge of Social Media[1], *"Companies need to realize that people who are front line and in direct contact with your customers are some of your most valuable assets if, data immediately in hand, they are empowered to rectify problems, answer questions, and delight customers during critical touch points."* Why hire an agency to handle your social media when your best social media spokespeople are **your people?**

Not only is it essential to understand how social platforms can be used for sales and marketing, it's important to grasp how they integrate with your other marketing efforts. Doing this well means you need to break social out of a silo and involve cross-functional teams. But that's not possible when you hire an outside team to manage social for you. In fact, such a move will hinder your ability to sync social with the rest of your marketing. The most innovative, forward-thinking companies have merged social, content and PR. By doing so, they can capitalize on the synergies between these three disciplines and eliminate any overlap between analysts, influencers, content authors and others.

Content–There's a reason content marketing has become all the rage in recent years. Without it, you have nothing to share with your target audience in the digital world. In other words, content underpins most–if not all–of your marketing efforts. But it's not enough to churn out content for content's sake. And it certainly no longer cuts it to pump out product- and company-focused content. The key to effective content marketing is to deeply understand and address your target audience's interests and concerns by publishing content in a variety of forms, in the channels where your audience spends time. Do this right and you'll lead more prospective buyers down the path to purchase, and more customers to long-term loyalty. Fail to do this, and you'll likely find yourself in the ranks of marketers who are wondering why their content marketing efforts are falling short.

Email Marketing–Email is not dead–not by a long shot. What has died, though, is faith in batch 'n' blast email campaigns. Marketers who believe that sending more and more emails to people on their lists is the answer to growing their businesses are becoming obsolete. Today's hybrid marketers are smarter. They're building much more personalized email campaigns, and they're creating dynamic experiences that guide the consumer along his journey to a purchase by incorporating great content, integrating social, and tapping into the right metrics to create engaging email messages.

SEO–To be a good hybrid marketer, you don't need to become an SEO (search engine optimization) expert. But you do need to have a basic grasp of how SEO strategies affect your content and your search rankings. Seattle-based search analytics company Moz offers a free Beginners Guide to SEO[2] that outlines how search engines operate, how consumers interact with them, and the basics of SEO design and development.

Analytics–If you're not measuring the effects of your marketing efforts, how can you prove your value? It's your job as a marketer to pull out actionable insights from your metrics: drops in traffic, high bounce rates, conversions, etc. Google Analytics[3] is the most obvious place to start if your company is not yet using monitoring analytics, and Search Engine Watch has one of the best intro to Google Analytics guides.[4]

If you're not a hybrid marketer, you don't have an umbrella view of how all the above marketing techniques work together to help you connect with consumers who aren't loyal to any one platform in an omni-channel world. My experience working at a marketing automation software company helped me become adept in every dimension, finding customers on social media one moment and on email the next. I learned a truly omni-channel approach–integrating email marketing, social media marketing, and all other marketing efforts. I learned the importance of being able to track each consumer's behavior across channels and in response to test various campaigns and marketing tactics to achieve better engagement and conversions.

Don't be a one-dimensional marketer–you're easily disposable.

1. http://www.bryaneisenberg.com/the-shake-weight-challenge-of-social-media/
2. http://moz.com/beginners-guide-to-seo
3. http://www.google.com/analytics
4. http://searchenginewatch.com/article/2243996/A-Guide-to-Getting-Started-With-Analytics

SIDE 1: CONTENT

"Content marketing is a marketing technique of creating and distributing valuable, relevant and consistent content to attract and acquire a clearly defined audience—with the objective of driving profitable customer action."–The Content Marketing Institute

Like any classic album, side one always includes the best songs, and the "hit". That's exactly what I've been doing here: opening up with content marketing and introducing the Big Rock concept, which I believe is the core of a successful content strategy. Side one is all about the why, the what and the how of content marketing. Everything I've learned by leading content strategies at both LinkedIn and Marketo, rolled into 18 chapters. This is the heart and soul of the book, and everything I know about kicking ass in the B2B space using content marketing.

Let's get started and drop the needle on side one, shall we?

CHAPTER 2

If Your Writing Sucks, So Will Your Content

If 2014 was the year of content marketing, then 2015 has to be the year of relevant content that doesn't suck.

The problem isn't necessarily content itself; it's the lack of quality content. Google's latest algorithm update is putting a stranglehold on the cookie-cutter, SEO-driven, keyword-stuffed, generic, regurgitated content that has become the white noise that blocks all of the quality content from surfacing. That's good news for the content marketers who "get it" by not focusing on creating more content, but on creating more relevant content.

Relevant content starts with understanding your audience

Let's face it—if you don't know who you're writing for, you're probably going to write something that misses the mark. Long gone are the days when buyers would suffer through company- and product-focused datasheets and other pieces. Now they want engaging, thoughtful content that relates to *their* business and *their* goals and challenges in whatever role they play within their companies. And they wouldn't mind being entertained in the process (yes, even businesspeople like to laugh and be distracted from the drudgery of the office once in a while).

You might not like what I have to say, but this means you need to roll up your sleeves and do some work to figure out just what makes your audience tick. You may hear this referred to as developing buyer personas or profiles. This is a step below creating audience segments, getting at the key individuals and roles within a company that you're trying to reach, engage and ultimately sell on your offering. Once you have a strong sense of what these people care about most, what motivates them to take action, and what type of information they're looking for on their journey to purchase, you'll be in a much better position to create relevant content.

Better writing will stand you apart—but it ain't easy

While there is no way we can all instantly become great content writers and producers, we can all go back and revisit what in my opinion seems to be the root of the "content relevance" problem. I remember reading a great post about hiring a journalist for your content marketing strategy. While that may be a good idea for creating topical, real-time, newsjacking-worthy content, I recommend just cutting to the chase and hiring a marketer who is interesting and writes well.

But that's just part of the puzzle. To be a good content marketer you have to have a personality that shines through and resonates with the audience. Have you ever met someone who lights up the room in person but then writes a piece of content that is more boring than watching paint dry? It happens because it's difficult to transfer a personality to paper.

Get some education and inspiration

Writing sucks, and it's hard. The people who enjoy writing are already making a living from it; they are called authors. The rest of us have to try a bit harder. So what's the answer? Start with the basics. Go read two or three books on becoming a better writer. Then read a comedian's autobiography for some tips on how to be funny. Maybe take a creative writing class. Then keep everything you learned from those sources in the back of your mind as you revisit your industry and your customer's needs.

Here are a few of the books I recommend:

- ***Everybody Writes: Your Go-To Guide to Creating Ridiculously Good Content***—The World's first Chief Content Officer, Ann Handley, delivers the owner's manual for really, really ridiculously good-looking content.

- ***It was the best of sentences; it was the worst of sentences***—June Casagrande—Who ever thought that a book about crafting strong sentences could be so vastly entertaining? Witty, smart, engaging, and instructive, this book has it all.

- ***The Book on Writing***—Paula LaRocque —A full lesson in becoming a better writer divided into three sections: A Dozen Guidelines to Good Writing, Storytelling, and Language and Writing Mechanics.

- ***Ernest Hemingway on Writing***–Larry W. Phillips–Amazing insights from one of America's greatest writers.
- ***Seinlanguage***–Jerry Seinfeld–The funniest man alive. Enough said.

Adding a fail-safe to your content creation process

While there's no magic formula to becoming a better writer, you can adopt some simple steps to help you improve. After you write a piece of content, read it out loud to yourself. If you find that you struggle to get through it, why should it be any different for your customers and prospects? If you do make it all the way through, ask someone else to read it. Then ask them three questions:

1. Was it helpful?
2. Was it interesting?
3. Will it inspire them to take action?

If the answer to each of these questions is yes, you probably have a solid piece of content on your hands... unless it's your mother giving you the feedback.

At the end of the day

I am not a writer, nor am I a journalist. What I do have going for me is the fact that I learn very quickly, I carry around a copy of *The Elements of Style*, I read as much as humanly possible, and I hate sleep. As content marketing continues to be a necessary tool for marketers of all stripes, let's all make a commitment to be better writers first and content creators second.

CHAPTER 3

The Blog is the Social Media Rug that Ties the Room Together

At the center of one of my favorite movies, *The Big Lebowski*, is a worn-out Oriental rug whose demise fuels a chain of hilarious events. After thugs relieve themselves on his rug, Jeffrey Lebowski—"the Dude"—laments to his friends: "Man, it really tied the room together." Indignant, he marches into the home of the other Jeffrey Lebowski and demands a replacement rug. It is, of course, promptly stolen.

I'd like to momentarily pose as a Film 101 professor and posit that the rug in *The Big Lebowski* is a metaphor. It represents the otherwise unambitious Dude's material aspirations. Like the Dude's rug, your blog is a symbol of your company's potential wealth. It's a form of social currency that, though perhaps not directly tied to your ROI, is certainly a harbinger of your future revenue. It's where all the marketing starts, your pivotal social media channel.

Yes, I said *social media channel*. Blogs aren't always thought of as part of a social media strategy, but I'd argue they are actually the most important part. As Brian Clark said on Copyblogger[1] in 2009 (a time when some social media marketers claimed the blog was dead):

At least once a year, various pundits declare ponderously that blogs are dead... usually killed by some platform that we label as "social media"... Those declarations are built, at least in part, on the mistaken notion that blogging and social media are different and distinct things.

The blog wasn't dead then, and it's not even close to dead now. More than ever, today's blogs function at the center of your social media strategy. They tie your online marketing "rooms" together, lending substance to your posts on other social media channels and referring readers to those channels.

Here are a few reminders as you create and maintain your company's blogging strategy:

- Content fuels social interaction, and that starts with your blog. Infusing your social channels with blog content captures attention. For example, when you link to a post on your blog from your LinkedIn Company page, you drive potential customers to your site.

- Authentic, well-written content counts. When conducting preliminary research, potential buyers look for original, well-written content that offers substantial information. By nature, blogs feature longer-form content, which offers deeper thought leadership. This content is your first step to engaging prospects.

- Remember the press release. The old-fashioned press release doesn't impact media as it used to, but the same kind of idea still lives on in your blog. Use it to announce new products, services, features, and other relevant company news with detail. Then, use your other social media outlets to tease viewers with content snippets that draw them back to your blog for full details. That way, you drive conversions right into your funnel. Because today's blog is far more versatile than yesterday's press release, it captures far more eyeballs.

- Always keep SEO in mind. Blogs significantly influence your search rankings. The metrics that search engines use just happen to be the exact same web elements that blog posts embody: fresh content and trending keywords that are relevant. The more your teaser social-media posts drive viewers to your blog, the stronger your blog's search engine authority.

Good content creates conversations, which lead to engagement and, ultimately, conversions. This is something I've seen time and time again through my experience and role with LinkedIn Influencer program's[2] enthusiastic thought leaders. Every day, brilliant minds like Deepak Chopra and Richard Branson share fresh ideas about marketing and business strategy. These leaders have placed a priority on sharing their thoughts in blog form because they know how powerful a brand-builder blogging can be.

While metrics don't necessarily credit your blog for conversions, every piece of content you post helps tie your marketing message together. Your posts capture the attention of search engines, build customer affinity, and feed every other social media channel you're engaged with. Like the perfect rug to underlie and compliment your furniture, everything starts with your blog.

My All-Time Favorite Blog and Why it's So Great

I've been asked a few times lately what I think makes a great blog post, so I thought I would share one of my all-time favorites. It's from Fred Wilson's very popular blog AVC[3]: musings of a VC in NYC. Wilson publishes one post per day, almost always on a topic related to venture capital entrepreneurship or the Internet.

This one in particular is absolutely brilliant. It's called Minimum Viable Personality[4] and is a guest post from a giant startup robot dinosaur that goes by FakeGrimlock[5]. In the tech startup world we often refer to the acronym MVP: Minimum Viable Product. MVP is basically the idea that, instead of trying to create a perfect new product, just get something out there and see if people actually like it, and then improve on it later. The "Grimster" has a different take on MVP, or Minimum Viable Personality as he calls it. Here he talks about the essential elements to building a successful product.

Here's a quick excerpt of the brilliant FakeGrimlock's post.[6]

PERSONALITY BETTER THAN MARKETING

WHEN CHOOSE PRODUCT, HUMANS ONLY CARE ABOUT DOES WORK, AND IS INTERESTING.

WORLD ALREADY FULL OF THINGS DO WORK. MOST BORING.

PERSONALITY = INTERESTING. INTERESTING = CARE. CARE = TALK.

EVERYONE CARE AND TALK ABOUT PRODUCT? YOU WIN.

FORMULA FOR WIN

The entire post is a perfect example of how to use text, images and personality to create a very special piece of content. You can read the entire post[7], and I highly encourage you to do so.

Why do I love this post so much? Because it includes all of the elements that make up a fantastic piece of content, including:

- It's a guest post, which is great for lending a new/unique voice to a blog.

- It's easy to read and contains no fluff. A great blog post has just enough words to make its point and leave you wanting more.

- It has personality. If you can't figure out how to inject personality into your blog, that's a huge problem.

- It has fantastic visuals. Great visuals don't have to cost a fortune; they just have to add value. The visuals used here are priceless.

- It's incredibly useful. This is something that I have printed out on my desk and celebrate daily. It's a constant reminder of how to be relevant and connect with your audience.

- It's inspiring, which is the most important element in my opinion. This post makes me want to be better at marketing and to share this advice with my network of fellow marketers. If your content can't inspire anyone to take action, then it is not doing what it's supposed to.

For more genius content from FakeGrimlock and Fred Wilson, you can follow them on Twitter: @FAKEGRIMLOCK[8] and @AVC[9].

1. http://www.copyblogger.com/blogs-social-media/
2. http://www.linkedin.com/today/posts?strategy=recentPosts
3. http://avc.com/
4. http://avc.com/2011/09/minimum-viable-personality/
5. https://twitter.com/FAKEGRIMLOCK
6. http://avc.com/2011/09/minimum-viable-personality/
7. http://avc.com/2011/09/minimum-viable-personality/
8. https://twitter.com/FAKEGRIMLOCK
9. https://twitter.com/avc

CHAPTER 4

The Blogging Food Groups

If you know me at all then you know that I am a huge fan of marketing analogies. One of my favorites, and most useful, is the blogging food groups. Originally coined by HubSpot's Rick Burns back in 2009, this is a strategy I have been applying for years. And I believe that it's more relevant than ever now that content marketing is such a vital part of the marketing mix.

A blog is different than a resource section. A resource section is a searchable, indexed library whereas a blog is a running narrative, a diary if you will, complete with posts.

As a major fuel source for social, it's vital to mix up the content on the blog; after all, variety is the spice of life. Just as anyone would quickly tire of eating from the same food group day after day, your customers and prospects can grow tired of consuming the same type of content again and again.

Burns recommends treating your blog like you would your diet, incorporating a healthy balance of content based on five food groups.

By providing a mix of how-to and influencer posts (whole wheat and grains), leadership articles and guest topics (vegetables), research and analysis (meats), light-hearted viral content (dessert and sweets) and bold statements (condiments), your blog will engage readers and, where applicable, hook potential customers. In fact, a recent HubSpot report[1] found that 82% of marketers who blogged daily saw an upswing in ROI.

For illustrative purposes I will run through an example of using the blogging food group strategy for a heavy metal blog.

Monday–You want to ease your audience back from the weekend with something light. Think 5 tips for this, how to's, etc. The example below is a practical "how-to" post that is a perfect way to start off the week.

How to Appreciate Heavy Metal

Edited by Rob S, Ben Rubenstein, Dave Crosby, Eric and 47 others

Edit Article

You might not be, or know someone who isn't into Metal, and want them to get into it, or to appreciate it yourself. These are some steps to get into it without becoming crazy, or upsetting others. Start out relatively easy; if you're into artists like Green Day, Good Charlotte, Mark Schultz, Third Day, Disciple, Skillet, or another rock group, then there are particular steps for you.

Tuesday—Time to get a bit heavier with your content and move onto the Spinach (good for you, even though it's a bit difficult to chew). In our example below, the author talks about how he can live vicariously through the dark themes from heavy metal instead of acting out those dark thoughts in real life. This is a thought-provoking piece from The Atlantic and a perfect example of Spinach content.

ENTERTAINMENT MAY 2011

How Heavy Metal Is Keeping Us Sane

Dark and disturbing, the music is honest about human nature

JAMES PARKER | APR 2 2011, 11:00 AM ET

5.7K

Share

267

Tweet

30

8+1

in

Share

More ▾

John P. Midgley/Corbis Outline

Wednesday—It's the middle of the week and time to give your audience something substantial, something to chew on for a bit. The Roast is a 1500–3000-word blog post on a topic that you want to own. Moz.com recently analyzed more than ten thousand blogs and found that in order to rank on page one within the search engines, your article or post should be a minimum of 1,500 words. The example below is a perfect one as it clocks in at 1,700 words, has lots of linkbacks and uses multimedia to add relevance.

THE HISTORY OF THE NEW WAVE OF BRITISH HEAVY METAL
by **Eduardo Rivadavia** May 8, 2014 2:24 PM

Thursday–Time to start a little fire. We call this post Tabasco: it's where you take a very strong view on a hot topic or call someone out. A great example is one I published on LinkedIn called "Is it OK to Drop the F-Bomb During a Keynote?". Check out the comments on that one. A little bit of controversy on the blog never hurt anyone, right? In the example below the author claims that five metal bands are better than Black Sabbath. (That's impossible–Black Sabbath invented Heavy Metal. I commented on this post numerous times!)

Metal

Five '70s Metal Bands Who Are Better Than Black Sabbath

By Nicholas Pell Thu., May 23 2013 at 3:05 AM
Categories: Metal

27 Comments

Like Share 214   Tweet 17   Pocket 8   8+1 0

Friday–My favorite day of the week and my favorite type of content: Chocolate Cake. This is fun content that can inject personality into your brand or business. You want to send your audience into the weekend with a smile on their face so that they will return on Monday. Think of a fun infographic (e.g., Kittens vs Bacon) or a fun top 10 list blog. The example below is simply curating funny reviews from Amazon on one of the most legendary albums of all time.

SUPPORTING YOUR LOCAL INDIE SHOPS SINCE 2007

THE FIRST FREE RECORD STORE FINDER APP JUST GOT A BIT MORE...KILLER.

VINYL District

ON THE FLY OR BEFORE YOU FLY

10 Hysterically Funny Reviews of Led Zeppelin IV by 10 People Who Hate It

BY JASON MILLER | AUGUST 16, 2011

By **A Customer**

This review is from: Led Zeppelin IV (aka ZOSO) (Audio CD)

Yes I know some people gave this album five stars but I've seen some five star reviews for the movie Howard The Duck here. I urge everyone not to believe people saying how great this album is. I think it's AWFUL. When I first heard it in 1986 I thought it was awful and fifteen years later I still do. Buy something else.

Since I love Friday Chocolate Cake content so much I thought I would share a second helping.

This blog idea came to me on a plane ride home from seeing Guns N' Roses in Las Vegas during their Appetite for Democracy run at the Joint. If I had to rank the top events in my life it would be number one, my wedding day, and number two, Guns N' Roses in Las Vegas.

While flying home slightly hungover from an epic weekend in Vegas, I started thinking of the enormously successful career that Axl Rose has had and what lessons his band could teach us content marketers. The result ended up as Chocolate Cake on the Marketo blog... but what would happen next completely blew my mind.

Guns N' Roses Shared my blog post!!!!!! That means that Axl Rose may or may not have seen my content!!!

Guns N' Roses @gunsnroses · 12 Dec 2012
Sure as hell never saw this coming - 5 Content Marketing Lessons from Guns N'
Rose bit.ly/12kqQmh via @marketo

Details   ↰ Reply ⇄ Retweet ★ Favorited Buffer Pocket ••• More

RETWEETS   FAVORITES
98   37

What did that Retweet do for Marketo? Well, nothing really. (Except for make an epic content story.) But it showed our audience that we had a personality and sent them into the weekend with a smile on their face. Ending the week on a high note our audience is very likely to return on Monday.

There you have it–the right diet to keep your readers satisfied and coming back for more.

1. http://cdn2.hubspot.net/hub/53/file-30889984-pdf/2013_StateofInboundMarketing_FullReport.pdf

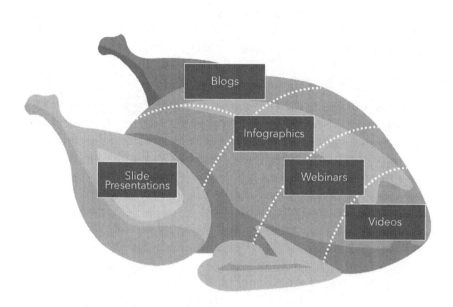

CHAPTER 5

What Does Content Marketing Have to do with Leftover Turkey? More Than You Think

A Brilliant Content Marketing Analogy; Thanksgiving Food for Thought, Literally.

A couple of years ago at Ad:Tech in San Francisco, I was lucky enough to score an interview with one of the smartest content marketers on the planet. Rebecca Lieb is an analyst at the Altimeter Group and author of Content Marketing. I asked her, "What's your number-one tip for companies who are struggling to produce enough content?"

She replied, "I use a Thanksgiving analogy. You cook up this giant bird to serve up on one glorious occasion and then proceed to slice and dice this thing for weeks on end. If you are like most families, you are going to be repurposing this bird as leftovers for quite some time, creating everything from sandwiches to soups and more. Your content marketing strategy can be thought of in the same way."

I love this analogy because it's easy to understand and even easier to explain to a content team. The idea here is to look for opportunities to repurpose the content that you already have. So where do you start? Look at your existing content and figure out how that can easily be re-purposed or sliced and diced into another smaller piece of content.

For example:

- Do you have webinars that can be turned into blog posts? There are many transcription services that can do this for you relatively cheaply. I have had great success using Transcription Star.

- Do you have white papers that you can turn into SlideShare presentations? When I was at Marketo we hired a design agency to turn a white paper into a self-guided visual journey for SlideShare. The white paper had 17,000 views. Not bad, right? Well the same content in a well-designed visual format garnered over 300,000. It's the same damn content just in a different form! (Remember that your customers and prospects are in control of where they consume your content, so you have to cater to the format and channel that they prefer.)

- Do you have evergreen content from last year that you can put a fresh coat of paint on, update a few numbers and re-release? I call this pre-loved content and it works because there's always a new audience waiting to rediscover great content; they might just be turned away by your self-imposed content expiration date.

- Do you have research reports that can be converted into infographics? Infographics can be a great way to tell a complex story very quickly and they are easy to share. More on that later.

- Don't forget about audio. Do you have content that could be repurposed into a podcast?

These are just a few ideas to get you started, but the point is to pull as much value as you can from one piece of content using bite-sized slices as teasers back to the original source. Not only does this give you additional content, in many cases it provides yet another channel where your content can be discovered.

This concept can be taken a step further and applied to what I refer to as "Big Rock" pieces of content, or content "Stake in the Ground." The current trend in content marketing is to develop an all-encompassing guide to whatever your keywords or topics are and write it strategically instead of instructionally. This type of content is very top of funnel and can serve many purposes such as SEO, fuel for social and lead generation, sales enablement, and event collateral, to name a few.

"Your Personal history is a part of what happens with your hands and your HEAD as you PLAY Music."

—Dave Grohl

CHAPTER 6

Not More Content, But More Relevant Content

Content marketing is no longer a game of numbers; it's now a game of relevance. You don't need to produce 75 blog posts a day to make an impact. The content farms are dead and for good reason. They were bloating the search results by stuffing keywords into poorly written content with only one purpose in mind: ranking on page one.

It's now vital for content marketers to understand that it's not more content that we need, but *more relevant* content. In fact, a recent study by the Chief Marketing Officer (CMO) Council[1] showed that 41% of overall respondents say they would consider ending a brand relationship because of irrelevant promotions, and an additional 22% say they would definitely defect from the brand.

Content marketers should change their mindset of writing for SEO and quantity to instead simply writing for their audience. Content marketing expert and author of Content Rules, Ann Handley, says it best:

"Focus on being useful to your customers. Create content that inspires—either creatively, or by data, or both. And make it enjoyable for your customers, with pathological empathy for their point of view. Your own point of view and perspective (or voice) really does come out of focusing relentlessly on your customers."

When it comes to empathizing with your customers and prospects, award-winning author and Inc. contributing writer Geoffrey James has come up with three ways to do this.

"In business, there are three levels of empathy. The first is "on-demand" empathy, which is the ability to sense what customers want. The second is "solution" empathy, which entails understanding a customer's problem and figuring out how to address it. The third is "transcendent" empathy where you create solutions to problems that customers don't even know that they have."

I like to think of this as moving from information to insights, as in "How can I take the information I have around my customers and prospects and use that to create more relevant content?". This concept can be taken a step further to develop what I refer to as a "Big Rock" piece of content. Big Rock content is our quarterly stake in the ground, if you will, or as Velocity Group's Doug Kessler calls it, your "one home run per quarter." I love Kessler's take on this:

"I feel that very soon content marketing is going to become a "home run" game. I know that's an American metaphor but what I mean is it will be about the big hits, the pieces that actually move markets as opposed to the background stuff that keeps you in the game. I think people are going to start learning that a few of those in any program changes everything, changes the dynamics of everything. It can make even a mediocre strategy look utterly brilliant if you just get a few winners in there. So people hopefully will be aiming higher."

I think it's time to stop "thinking like a publisher" as so many content marketing experts recommend and start "publishing like a publisher." Ask yourself what conversation you want to own and then write the all-encompassing guide and take on that conversation better than your competitors. Find out the most pressing questions asked by your customers and prospects and then write the book on it literally. But don't overdo it with a bunch of fluff; you have to avoid the urge to talk about yourself too much and write strategically instead of instructionally (meaning, don't make it a huge instruction manual).

If you want to own a conversation, then you need to do it bigger and better than your competition. If the topic is a busy one, then you need to find a unique angle of your own and go straight for the jugular. Take a few shots, take a few risks, and shake things up.

There's Too Much Value in This Content, Said No One Ever

A great example of Big Rock content is Marketo's Definitive Guide series. They have created a series of eBooks clocking in at close to 100 pages each. A couple of years ago while I was at Content Marketing World, someone walked up to me (at the time I worked at Marketo) and said, "Hey man, I love your content at Marketo, I love the Definitive Guides, but I have to tell you that it's just too much content—there's too much value there."

I immediately thought to myself, "Are you out of your mind?" What marketer has ever downloaded something and thought there is too much value here? No marketer. This person had a very short-sighted view of this piece of content. What this person didn't realize is that the Definitive Guides are something that was repurposed using the Turkey analogy mentioned previously. Out of this one Big Rock piece of content, we had carved out 25 blog posts, two infographics, two webinars, two videos, two SlideShare presentations, and some cheat sheets. The list goes on and on; it's all about what you can imagine to pull out of the thing. In other words, Big Rock content is the foundation that can fuel your campaigns for quite some time.

The bottom line is that B2B marketers are going to need to start repurposing in order to scale. After all, 73% of them are producing more content than they did one year ago and 58% plan to increase their content marketing budget over the next year. With the increase in budget, it's easy enough to find partners and agencies to help. Since this is primetime for 2016 planning, it's the perfect time to start considering how you can repurpose your existing content for new channels, campaigns, and initiatives in the coming year.

Marketo creates one Big Rock Definitive Guide per quarter; it's their home run, if you will. Basically they create the "Definitive Guide to Whatever the Hell Conversation They Want to Own" in the marketing space, and the results are tremendous.

And it's scalable. Creating one Big Rock per quarter can be a very powerful content strategy as you quickly build up an arsenal of gated content for lead gen as well as a resource section on your website.

I think there is a tendency to overcomplicate this process. I've seen waterfall models for content strategy that look more complicated than the plans for a nuclear reactor. The truth is that many brands and companies are nowhere near that sophisticated or ready for a strategy of that magnitude. It's quite frightening to see these types of models put in front of a team of marketers who are early on in the content planning phase. I believe it scares them away from actually diving in with both feet, not to mention trying to get buy-in on something they can't even wrap their head around. My advice is to keep it simple by starting with one piece of substantial content that can then be plugged into a basic demand-gen model.

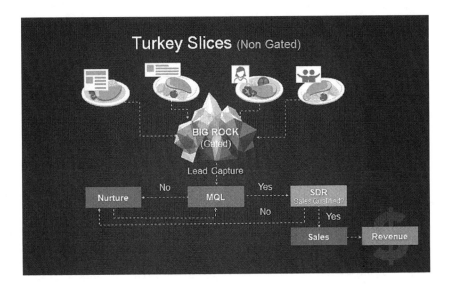

That's where Big Rock content comes into play. This is a substantial investment in one big piece of relevant content that is your stake in the ground and can fuel your demand gen, social and content strategy for up to an entire quarter. It's a definitive guide to whatever it is that your company or product does. For example, when I started at LinkedIn close to a year ago, my job was to tell the story of the marketer, specifically the content marketer, and how they should be using LinkedIn as part of their overall integrated marketing strategy. So I developed The Sophisticated Marketer's Guide to LinkedIn[2]: the all-encompassing, one-stop shop to marketing on LinkedIn, written both strategically AND instructionally.

Big Rock Content: The Why

- **Answering Questions for Prospects and Customers**–As I mentioned previously, this is the core and the main purpose of the guide: to help not sell. The more you make this about the customer or prospect and less about your business, the more successful your Big Rock will be.

- **SEO**–Even though the Big Rock is a gated piece of content, the page that it lives on in the resources section or blog is going to be rich with content. The Turkey Slices will be ungated and, if done right, drive traffic back to the page and provide linkbacks.

This can be a very powerful way to signal to the search engines that you are an authority on this topic.

- **Fuel for Social and Demand Gen**—One Big Rock piece of content and the accompanying Turkey Slices can fuel both social and demand gen for a full quarter and even longer based on the topic. The broader the topic, the longer the shelf life.

- **Influencer Marketing**—If you want to get to an influencer's audience, you need to approach these authorities with the mentality of "What can I do for you?". The Big Rock is a perfect opportunity for you to reach out and invite the influencers in your space to be a part of your content strategy. When reaching out, get to your point very quickly and make it as easy as possible for them to contribute either a quote or by answering a few questions via a quick email interview. When influencers see you extend their reach, they are likely to reciprocate by sharing your content with their audience. At the very least, they are almost certain to share their contribution to your Big Rock with their followers.

- **Lead Gen**—While your Big Rock is gated, Turkey Slices act as tentacles out in the social and demand-gen world, leading people back to the gated content even if they aren't ready to give you their info. The Turkey Slices will act as teasers and help you stay top of mind until these folks are ready to take the next step.

- **Owning the conversation**—At the end of your Big Rock run, and if you follow all of this advice and stick to the "always-on" approach moving forward, there is a very good chance that you will "own" the conversation around your topic of choice. Along with "ownage" comes influence, which can quickly turn to thought leadership. That's the Holy Grail for marketers.

1. http://www.curata.com/resources/ebooks/ultimate-guide-to-content-curation
2. The Sophisticated Marketer's Guide to LinkedIn

"IT's Not who does it first, it's who does it best."

— David Bowie

CHAPTER 7

Three Ways to Create a Big Rock

The Big Rock concept works no matter how big or small your marketing team is, but you will need to have a budget. It's doesn't have to be a lot, but remember that you get out of the Big Rock what you put into it. Over the years I have found three very easy and effective ways to create a Big Rock; which one you choose depends on where you can get a big early win. If possible, I recommend starting simple by answering the biggest question your prospects are asking. Just remember that one might take a bit more time while the others are quicker wins since you will pull from existing content.

So let's dive into the three ways to create your Big Rock.

1. **Use What You Have**—If you have a blog, then you have Big Rock content waiting in the wings. Find a theme around a number of blog posts and tie them together. Taking a page from the Blogging Food Groups mentioned previously is a great way to create a theme around one topic but come at it from different angles.

Example: Frolic in the Snow with those 'in the know'—This Big Rock was pulled together using content that already existed in the LinkedIn Influencer Marketing Channel.[1]

2. **Base it on Keyword Research**—Using a bit of keyword research, figure out how prospects and customers are talking about your brand or service and then simply answer those questions with one all-encompassing guide. If you need help with keyword research, I recommend hiring a pro such as www.moz.com or the very smart folks at www.toprankonlinemarketing.com. This is a very good investment. If you are looking for a quick and dirty way to find the exact topics for a Big Rock, try using my favorite, Ubersuggest[2]. Or for LinkedIn-specific content, there is a great solution called Trending Content (just keep in mind that it is platform specific). For more suggestions, check out Internet Marketing Ninjas' post on free keyword research tools[3].

Example: LinkedIn – The Sophisticated Marketer's Guide[4]

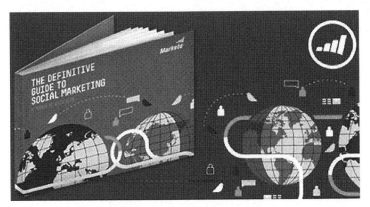

Example: Marketo – The Definitive Guide to Social Marketing[5]

3. Flip Your Case Studies on Their Heads—Case studies are traditionally considered to be bottom funnel content, but with a simple twist they can effectively be turned into top of funnel content. By simply grouping together several of these "case studies" and changing case study to success story, you get a whole new way to promote this content at the top of the funnel.

Example: Pantheon—8 Amazing Drupal Launches[6]

Treat the "Big Rock" like a product launch

This is a vital first step in the process and often the most difficult. Those who know me well know that I am not a big fan of planning ahead as I like to move quickly and create content on the fly. But this is key—if your Big Rock idea sucks or doesn't get buy-in from execs and product folks, you are in for a long road of painful back and forth.

The Outline

This is the very first step in the process. You are basically creating a table of contents that will serve as the introduction to the Big Rock and also as an intro to stakeholders for early buy-in/feedback, etc.

The Executive Overview

This is three or four PowerPoint slides that complement your outline and give your execs a snapshot of the who/what/why and how of the content.

Be sure to include the following in your executive overview:

Overview

Target audience
B2B Marketers

What is the unmet need?
An all-encompassing guide to using LinkedIn to drive and foster thought leadership.

How will members/customers find it?
Email campaign, social promotion, influencer outreach, webinar, and blog. Both organic and paid promotion.

How will members/customers share it?
Social networks and email.

Marketing Strategy

Approach/timeline
Guide completed timeline/global launch timeline

Channel and creative strategy
Where will this content live and how will it be promoted?

Creative
Concepts and creative, internal or external

Goals and KPIs

Objective
Drive MQLs (Marketing Qualified Leads) and adoption

Success metrics
xxx Downloads in first 30 days, xxx MQLs, views, influencer mentions, etc.

Line up Partners/Agencies

You don't have to go at this alone and, if you have the budget, I recommend that you outsource part of this process. There are agencies/vendors that can help with the writing, editing, design, interviews, etc. In essence, you can rally an entire team to create an epic Big Rock. I don't recommend putting all your eggs in one basket when it comes to an agency, so find a core of agency/writers/ contractors that understand your business, the space you operate in, and your goals and stick with them. That's how to scale.

Socializing your Big Rock idea/plan

Build a list of the internal stakeholders who need to approve and sign off on the outline. Are you missing any major topics, is there anything you can cut? I tend to throw the entire kitchen sink into these outlines because your baby will likely be unrecognizable when you get it back based on the number of folks who will be adding their two cents. A good content marketing manager will be able to convey to the stakeholders the importance of keeping this concise and prevent it from turning into a giant instruction manual.

Internal stakeholders to socialize your outline with will likely include:

Marketing: VPs, Directors, Managers—These folks will likely need to sign off on the final version so it's important to keep them in the loop along the way.

Product Marketing—Be very clear that you are asking for their suggested feedback, but that you do not want this to turn into a product manual or instructional booklet.

Callout: The Big Rock needs to be written strategically AND instructionally, though with less focus on the latter. "What happens when you get an instruction manual? You throw it in the trash and go to YouTube." –Brian Solis

Global Marketing Leads—This is VITAL. US-based content marketing managers have a really bad habit of not thinking globally from the very start. Your geos are your friends and you will need their support for a successful global launch. But more on that later.

Brand Review—I can't tell you how many times I've been chased around by the "brand police" in regards to content not meeting their requirements or missing the mark by using the wrong logo, etc. My recommendation is to make sure each of your vendors, designers and agencies is using the latest approved color palettes and logos.

When socializing the outline with your internal stakeholders, it is important to put in very specific due dates for feedback. If they miss that date, it's time to move on. A piece of content of this size has a lot of moving parts to it; one missed deadline can throw a wrench in the entire process. Be stern, specific, and most importantly, meet your deadlines and keep this thing moving forward.

Include thought leader quotes and interviews for third-party validation

Since you are creating the "definitive" guide on your topic, it's important to include voices outside of yours for validation. Don't forget that this guide's main purpose is to help, not sell. As social and content expert Jay Baer says, "the difference between helping and selling is only two letters" and "Sell something, get a customer for a day; help someone, get a customer for life."

Just as I've done in this book, the addition of thought leaders in the form of interviews and quotes strategically placed throughout your guide is a great way to add helpful content while validating your message and purpose. This doesn't have to be a complicated process and can lead to fantastic content that can be repurposed using the Turkey analogy, which we learned about in chapter 5.

For the Sophisticated Marketer's Guide, I hired an agency to help come up with the questions and field the interviews for me. I chose to interview five thought leaders in the space and use similar questions for each. Using three of the same questions and two thought leader-specific ones can lend a nice flow to the guide. Plus, you can later repurpose those interviews into blog content, i.e., thought leaders all answering the same question. It's "Five thought leaders' take on a topic or question" and this can be super valuable when promoting the full guide using the rolling thunder approach that I discuss later in the book.

The Design

I'm not a fan of templates as they tend to lead to conformity. Let's be honest, template guides can be downright boring. If you are putting a significant effort into a Big Rock piece of content, do not let the design suffer. In this day and age you have mere seconds to grab one's attention (see chapter 10 for more on this). In fact, the design is going to play a major role in your success. And it will be the basis for each of the assets that is created to promote your Big Rock. So don't skimp on the design. Make it one with the content.

Take it Global

During the outline process, you should have been reaching out to give your global marketing leads a heads up to start thinking about which thought leaders, case studies, etc. they would like to include. When doing so, DO NOT refer to this as them "repurposing content" but instead make them part of the process. I learned very quickly that it's vital as a content marketer to always have a global vision in mind for every piece of content from conception through translation all the way to delivery. This includes using universally global images and references throughout. Doing so will set you up very nicely when you get the final version of the core content for your Big Rock and start the translation and regionalization of your content. I would recommend a minimum two-week buffer once the final Big Rock is created for each region to translate and localize.

If you don't have marketing counterparts in the different geos where your company operates or if there are only sales folks, it's important to keep them in the loop on what's coming so that they can be best trained on how to use the content. If your Big Rock is a research piece, be sure to create an executive summary of 3-4 editable PowerPoint slides that they can easily customize and include in their pitches to clients.

When translating your content for other markets, I can tell you that no matter how great your US agency is, there will be translation errors when working with international translators—and that can quickly become frustrating to those involved. I recommend taking the content as far as you can and then finding a translator locally. One option I have heard great things about is Cloudwords.[7]

Leading a content initiative from the US and not over-communicating with your leads can very quickly make them feel disconnected from your plans and make it much more difficult to get them on board later on. Always over-communicate and take their feedback on every aspect of your Big Rock; these folks need to be on board and you need them to want your Big Rock to be a global success. But more on that coming up in a later chapter as I give you my five lessons learned from doing this many times.

Big Rock Bells and Whistles (Nice-to-Haves for Your Big Rock)

The List—Conclude your Big Rock with a list of Top 10 or Top 20 influencers in that topic or space. List their Twitter handles, LinkedIn profiles, etc. This can include folks that you interviewed for your guide but it's more of a resource for the audience so that they can get a jumpstart if they are looking to expand their knowledge even further. This is also great for what we call "ego bait" and will likely garner additional shares from the folks who are included.

Data Points—Pepper in data points or mini infographics that support your overall theme or topic. If you want to use an infographic created by someone else, reach out and ask for permission. Most people are pretty cool with this as long as you give credit and/or a linkback.

Thought Leader Quotes—I recommended earlier that you should include interviews with thought leaders. Here I'm talking about a similar concept, but instead of full interviews, use only quotes. There are two ways to go about this: one is to tell a set of thought leaders that you would really love to have them contribute to your guide and ask them to provide a quote. The second is to find and pull quotes from existing content on the web and just let them know after it's published. They should be flattered.

1. http://marketing.linkedin.com/blog/a-holiday-gift-of-marketing-inspiration-from-linkedin/
2. http://ubersuggest.org/
3. http://www.internetmarketingninjas.com/blog/content/free-keyword-research-tools-search-sug-gestions/
4. http://marketing.linkedin.com/blog/introducing-the-sophisticated-marketers-guide-to-linkedin/
5. http://www.marketo.com/definitive-guides/social-marketing/
6. http://www.slideshare.net/GetPantheon/pan-8-amazingdrupallaunchesr2
7. http://www.cloudwords.com/

CHAPTER 8

Launching Your Big Rock

The "Bat out of Hell" Approach—Even though this record came out when I was three years old, I very much respect the fact that it is one of the best-selling albums in the history of recorded music. It has sold over 43 million copies worldwide, is ranked number 343 on Rolling Stone magazine's 500 greatest albums of all time, and continues to be an amazing catalog seller all the way up to today. How did this happen? The band and their record label have an "always-on" approach to marketing. This same type of thinking is vital for content marketers today. There was the album release, the tour, the singles, the radio play, the record sales and even today Amazon will likely suggest this album to you or remind you that you don't have it in your rock 'n' roll collection and retarget the hell out of you until you buy it. That's the lesson for content marketers: just stay top of mind with little reminders until you get your customers and prospects to the next step in their journey. Much like Meatloaf, it may take several touch points to move your audience along. And even when they do take that first step, they will likely need a few more to become a customer. Then it's time to cross-sell and upsell. Ever heard of the Meatloaf fan club?

Just as with any product launch, it's important to come out of the gates swinging and with all guns a'blazin'. Fire your big cannons (Email and Blog Announcement) and then switch to air cover for strategic strikes (Social Channels, Paid Amplification, Native Advertising, Influencer Outreach). Make sure you have the following lined up and ready to go. I recommend creating a simple run-of-show doc as a checklist for your big day. Time it out over the course of the launch day for a rolling thunder approach, then plan out your always-on strategy.

- **Landing page**—The golden gate to your Big Rock. Don't skimp on design and keep the fields on the form to only what is necessary. Marketo's research shows a $10 drop in cost per lead when shortening a form from nine fields to five.

- **Blog**—The blog announcement directing to the landing page is the introduction of your Big Rock to the world. But have additional Turkey Slices lined up to roll out the following weeks: thought leader interviews from the guide, snippets from other parts of the Big Rock, etc.

- **Email drop**—Schedule the email drop to go live only after the blog announcement is live and you have tested your lead form to make sure it's working properly. A very cool thing we do at LinkedIn is send a follow-up InMail to the folks that didn't open the original. We've had great success combining this with some basic A/B testing of subject lines.

- **Social posts** with custom images. Don't forget to include unique source tags, or UTM parameters[1], for tracking each channel. You can do this simply by adding a custom query to the end of the link.

For example:

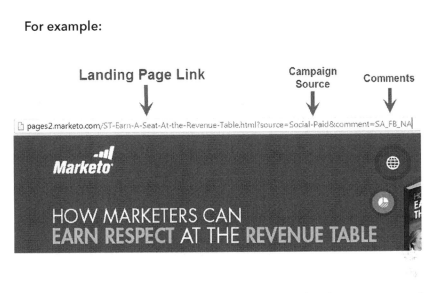

Measuring this requires the ability to create landing pages and tracking codes for each asset, a capability found in your marketing software.

- **Native advertising**–Organic is good, paid is better. Make sure to set some budget aside for social media advertising in the form of sponsored posts. More on this in chapter 28.

- **Influencer outreach**–There are two ways to ask the influencers included in your Big Rock to share it with their audience. The first is to send them an advance copy of your Big Rock (have your designer include a large "DRAFT ONLY" on the front of the content to keep it from going public early) giving them a heads up that they are included. Also include a paragraph or two of suggested copy (in case they would like to blog about it) and a few suggested social sharing messages. When dealing with influencers in your space, you need to make this as easy as possible for them to share as they are likely VERY busy. The second way to reach out to the influencers is to simply craft an email with one or two lines (keep it short and to the point!!!) telling them why you think it's relevant to them or their audience and what you would like them to do with it. If you included a quote from them or mentioned them in the Big Rock, there's a great chance they will share it. If not, then simply send them the same note asking if they would like to participate in your next content piece.

- **Press release**—If your company is privately funded, issue a press release about your new Big Rock. If your company is public, then your blog post is your press release.

- **Message to global team**—Craft an email and have it ready to go the morning of the Big Rock launch to your entire organization. Include a couple of sample social sharing messages and ask everyone to share the Big Rock with their social networks. Don't forget to give a special shout out to all those on your team who played a role in the Big Rock and those who will support this piece of content moving forward.

- **Message to sales**—Super important and often overlooked. Send a note to your sales reps and sales development team. I recommend including a drafted email that they can easily personalize and send to their customers and prospects along with a link to the ungated asset. That way the folks they already have relationships with won't have to fill out a form.

Plan out the year

The Big Rock content is not only awesome, it's also scalable. Once you get through the process of creating and launching your first Big Rock, it's time to start thinking about the next one. Choose a different keyword, topic, or additional group of case studies for each quarter. Plan ahead with design, concept, theme, writers, thought leaders to include, etc.

For example, when I started at LinkedIn, the number-one question from the audience I was targeting (marketers) was simply "How do I market my business, product or service on LinkedIn?" To answer that question I created The Sophisticated Marketer's Guide to LinkedIn: a one-stop shop for everything a marketer needs to know to be successful with marketing on LinkedIn. Keep in mind that this piece of content is very top of funnel so it doesn't go into too many details or sales pitches. Instead it's answering questions about marketing on LinkedIn, providing expert advice, and driving overall awareness of LinkedIn Marketing Solutions.

As I mentioned before, the Big Rock is scalable. Based on the success of The Sophisticated Marketer's Guide I am already in the process of creating the next two in the series: The Sophisticated Marketer's Guide to Thought Leadership and The Sophisticated Marketer's Guide to Content Marketing. Both play off the original, but each owns its respected topics and will be major content pieces to drive both awareness and adoption of thought leadership and content marketing on LinkedIn. While they will not be as lengthy as the original, they will be substantial 30-page ebooks that cover the topics thoroughly.

The Results

Without sounding too much like a miracle product or late night infomercial, I will tell you that I personally have seen tremendous success with Big Rock content. The Sophisticated Guide I created for LinkedIn Marketing Solutions drove an incredible $4.6 million of business in the first half of 2014. That's from ONE piece of content, my friends. The total cost for the project was around $25,000. I won't even tell you the ROI on that because that would be gloating. But, I am proud to say it won a Killer Content Award at the B2B Content2Conversion Conference[2] and honorable mention from the Content Marketing Institute awards.[3]

The really interesting thing to note though was what channel drove those results and what levers we could pull along the way when we needed an extra boost. Using the "Bat out of Hell" approach to launching your content like a product, you can see the results from the first two weeks below.

In this type of "always-on" strategy, you will quickly see a shift from the email being the leading driver of marketing qualified leads to the blog taking over and then that being surpassed by native advertising (in this case Sponsored Updates). The reason being is that the Turkey Slices provide a rolling thunder approach by utilizing the blog and native advertising, all driving traffic back to the Big Rock.

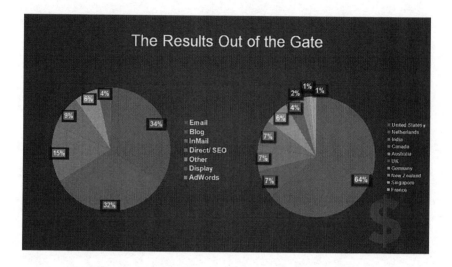

It's a beautiful thing and almost self-sustaining. This always-on approach can fuel your social channels and demand gen for at least a full quarter and likely longer. Once you squeeze all the value from one Big Rock, it's time to move on to the next conversation you want to own.

Anyone can do this and it will work for any industry. You may not get the same results, but you will get positive results if you follow this process and execute it well. Want more proof this works? At Marketo, each Definitive Guide drove around half a million dollars in revenue during my time there. Jon Miller, the VP of Marketing there (no relation by the way) is very transparent with Marketo's metrics. Check out any one of his amazing Secret Sauce presentations[4] where Jon shows the exact numbers. It's quite impressive.

While that's only the revenue side of the benefits of the Big Rock– and in my opinion, the most important–you can realize many more benefits by creating a piece of content of this magnitude. This includes:

SEO–This Big Rock piece of content will show the search engines that you mean business. As long-form content is indexed, it will likely drive linkbacks. Linkbacks show authority and result in higher search engine rankings. As mentioned before, the Turkey Slices will also help drive links and referral traffic to support the overall SEO goal as well.

Fuel for Social Channels–The Big Rock and its repurposed assets can be a great source of content for each of your channels. On LinkedIn specifically, I repurposed The Sophisticated Guide into almost 20 different assets, from infographics and webinars to blog posts, videos, and more. While the Big Rock was gated for lead gen, each of the repurposed smaller, snackable assets was not gated. I think of these as tentacles, if you will, out in the social world, all leading back to the gated Big Rock. If someone isn't ready to give us their info (i.e., fill out a form), they will likely still come across one or two of our smaller repurposed Turkey Slices and eventually fill out the form. It's all about staying top of mind, which you do by repurposing the Big Rock.

Sales Collateral–The sales team and agency partners have a nice piece of collateral to share with their clients, keeping them informed and continuing the conversation.

Giveaways for Events–A printed version of the Big Rock is a fantastic giveaway for events as well.

Tools used for developing the Big Rock:

Google Docs[5]–For general outline and full, global go-to-market plan.

Box[6]–For storing and easily sharing design, concepts, videos and turkey slices (i.e., repurposed materials).

Curata[10]–For planning, scheduling and measuring the pipeline impact of your Big Rock and related content.

Resources/ Agencies used for the Big Rock:

Ten Ton Marketing[7]–Stephanie Tilton - Writer/Editor

Scorch[8]–Agency for concept, layout, design and repurposing of materials. (i.e., Turkey Slices)

TopRank Online Marketing[9]–Agency for SEO consulting, conducting interviews, and writing blog content to support the Big Rock (i.e., Blogging Food Groups).

1. https://support.google.com/analytics/answer/1033867?hl=en
2. http://content2conversion.com/the-killer-content-awards/
3. http://www.contentmarketingawards.com/
4. http://www.slideshare.net/marketo/marketing-secret-sauce-scottsdale-june-2014
5. https://docs.google.com/document/u/0/?pli=1&showDriveBanner=true#
6. https://box.com
7. http://www.tentonmarketing.com
8. http://scorchagency.com
9. http://www.toprankmarketing.com
10. http://www.curata.com/

"We believed that anything that was worth doing was worth Overdoing..."

—Steven Tyler

CHAPTER 9

Keep on Rolling

Now that we've covered developing the Big Rock in great detail and shared the end results, let's talk about how we got there and how you know it's time to move on. Based on the size of your target audience, as I mentioned before, one Big Rock piece of content can easily fuel your demand gen and social channels for up to a quarter and in many cases much longer. Keep in mind though that the broader the topic, the longer the shelf life of your content. In my experience at both Marketo and LinkedIn I have seen Big Rocks keep on keepin' on for an entire year, or longer, and continue to drive leads.

When do you know you have a hit on your hands? You should have a sense of how your Big Rock will perform right out of the gate. Set a goal for 30-60-90 days and stick to it. For example, at LinkedIn we set a first-30-days goal of x number of downloads and x number of MQLs. The Turkey Slices that you re-purpose from the Big Rock will be the main driver of your "always-on" approach. Schedule one slice to run on the blog every week as part of a rolling thunder approach but mix it up. Try an interview with a thought leader from the Big Rock one week, then an infographic, then a SlideShare, then back to a blog post. All of these un-gated teasers driving back to the Big Rock will keep it top of mind with your customers and prospects while adding fuel to your social and demand-gen programs.

A month or so after your initial launch you can start sending the Turkey Slices in email campaigns to those who either didn't open the original email or download the guide through some other channel. If you reach your first goal date and look to be falling short, take a look at what levers you can pull to turn up the heat. If the conversation that you're trying to own is related to a new or innovative product, service offering or business model, you will likely be able to segment your target audience according to an early adopter bell curve. Your first wave of responders likely falls into the innovators or early adopters segments.

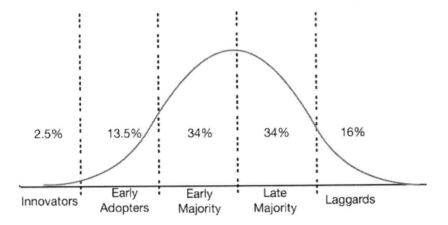

Figure 1 Everett M. Rogers Bell Curve from Diffusion of Innovations, the landmark 1962 textbook that popularized the study of how new ideas and technologies spread through societies, early adopters make up 13.5% of the consumers who will adopt an innovation.

When you feel as though you've saturated that audience and have succeeded at educating them on your Big Rock topic, there will likely be another audience right behind them, that of the early majority, who is now ready to receive your message. Depending upon your business and the conversation you are trying to own, this segmentation could fall along industry/vertical lines, e.g., Technology and Media companies first, Retail and Manufacturing next, with Oil and Gas, and State and Local Government last. Once it appears that you have saturated that segment, move on to the late majority and finally to the laggards.

Even though you will likely feel like you've played this song to death, there will be an entirely new audience for whom this content is groundbreaking.

Know when to hold 'em, know when to fold 'em

How do you know when your Big Rock has served its purpose and it's time to retire? Just as Motley Crüe decided to go out on their own terms with a final tour, your content should go out on a high note on its own terms before it loses all of its appeal. If your Big Rock starts to suffer from overexposure, then it's time to archive it onto your resource center. It's vital to keep this content piece alive and kicking and preserve all of the SEO goodness that you have driven, but just remove it from your inbound and outbound channels for now. Hopefully you have been building your next Big Rock which can take over where this one left off, or even begin an entirely new journey around the next conversation you want to own.

Also keep in mind that this may be a great candidate for a version 2.0 with a fresh coat of paint and some updated chapters as you think about repurposing content moving forward.

Measuring your Big Rock success over time

As you build out your arsenal of Big Rock content, you'll want to measure the impact of each asset on your business. Here are just a few of the ways you can analyze how your content is performing over time:

- Measuring month-over-month growth in organic website traffic, downloads, and MQLs. Organic traffic is an important metric here because it reflects the people who are finding your website by means other than paid promotion or direct brand awareness (i.e., typing in your URL or searching your brand names). Track how much of that traffic converts into leads, and be sure to tag the lead source properly so you can see whether those leads turn into pipeline and revenue.

- Lead generation by channel. Track lead generation by source to determine which ones are driving the most traffic. It can also be insightful to track how these vary by product line or business unit. Measuring this requires the ability to create landing pages and tracking codes for each asset, which you can do using your marketing software. As your content arsenal grows, you can take this a step further by measuring what kinds of content drive the most leads and which content pieces ultimately drive the most revenue.

- Number of Resources Published (Big Rocks and Turkey Slices)— Keep a running dashboard of the various eBooks, case studies, infographics, white papers, webinars, etc. that you create and publish along with the target audience, vertical, and persona. As your content library grows, this will be a great way to quickly identify any holes in your content strategy while having everything in one place, well organized so your sales teams can grab what they need, when they need it, without jumping through hoops.

The Encore

As with any great performance, the encore is based upon the audience's reaction and willingness to stick around for one last hoorah. Here are two excellent encore opportunities for your Big Rock:

- **Third-party lists**—There are a ton of paid opportunities to get your Big Rock in front of the audience of other relevant outlets. For example, a B2B marketer could pay to send their Big Rock out to the MarketingProfs database. It's a great way to reach a new audience while delivering your message from a trusted source outside of your own brand.

- **Nurture programs**—The Big Rock and its various Turkey Slices can easily be dropped into relevant nurture campaigns and help awaken some leads that may not have been served this content the first time around.

CHAPTER 10

The Importance of Going Visual

We are all visual thinkers. 75% of the sensory neurons in our brains process visual information. As prospects and customers continue to be bombarded with information in the form of pure text such as white papers and blogs, it can be difficult to differentiate your content from the competition. Visual content can help.

Stanford scholar and author Robert E. Horn explains in his book *Visual Language* that incorporating visual elements with writing to show and tell simultaneously has many benefits. Visual language aids in decision making, is more persuasive, and makes a better, longer-lasting overall impression than simple text. Think about the implications and opportunities for a marketer, especially in this incredibly fast-paced world of social. With attention spans shorter than ever before, you have mere seconds to grab your customers' and prospects' attention. In fact, The National Center for Biotechnology Information reports that the average attention span of a human being dropped from 12 seconds in 2000 to 8 seconds in 2013. To put that into perspective, the attention span of a goldfish is 9.

It's no wonder that visual content is at an all-time high. Social media sites that focus exclusively on images are swiftly gaining in popularity. In February 2013, TechCrunch reported that the percentage of online adults using Pinterest (15%) had almost caught up[1] to the percentage using Twitter (16%). Facebook recognized that Instagram was going places when it purchased the photo-focused app for $1 billion in 2012. As of March 2014, Instagram has 200 million monthly active users. Facebook, Twitter, and LinkedIn all get *the power of the picture* and have added better image-sharing functionality to their platforms over the past few years.

The Image is the New Headline

A famous quote from the father of advertising, David Ogilvy, says, "On the average, five times as many people read the headline as read the body copy. When you have written your headline, you have spent eighty cents out of your dollar." I think this statement holds true today, but with the insertion of a visual element as the new headline. For example, I have seen many instances of text-based content repurposed into a visual format and achieving 10–15 times more views than the original. That is a game changer in the world of content marketing.

Buyers and prospects are now in control, choosing the way in which they consume content. If they are searching on SlideShare[2] or Pinterest for information about your company, your content in those channels better be in the format that they prefer. This means infographics[3], interactive presentations, videos and other visual assets need to be a part of your overall integrated content marketing strategy, helping to fuel your social channels.

Repurpose What You Have

You might be thinking to yourself, 'How in the hell am I going to produce all of this new visual content? All I have are boring white papers.' This is the perfect time to call upon the great suggestion for repurposing content I shared with you earlier from Altimeter Group analyst Rebecca Lieb: "I love using the turkey analogy. People really get that. You start out with the turkey at Thanksgiving and that's the main event, and then everybody knows that after Thanksgiving you're eating turkey sandwiches, you have turkey on your salad, and maybe a little turkey hash. Journalists very quickly learn how to treat their stories and their sources like that turkey. That's not meant to sound derogatory, but you need to understand what your content assets are and how and when to use them."

The Turkey analogy from Chapter 5 can easily be applied to visual content as well. Reimagining your existing content and interpreting it into a visual medium not only solves this problem, it breathes new life into your existing content. If you are strapped for bandwidth or resources or just aren't sure where to start, you can engage some really good, affordable creative agencies that specialize in doing just this sort of thing.

Rock 'n' Roll Design Doesn't Have to Cost a Fortune

A couple of visual platforms that I love to use that are either free or have pricing plans for every budget include:

For SlideShare: Canva[4], Haiku Deck[5], Prezi[6]

For infographics: Easel.ly, Piktochart, Visual.ly

If you have the budget and want an absolute home run with a full PR strategy, nobody beats Column Five Media[7]. These guys are the best in the business.

Go Visual or Go Home

The challenge of visual content marketing is to find the right mix of words, illustrations, and designs to capture a subject and make it memorable and more easily understood. Adding an element of fun can go a long way as well (think kittens and bacon). At the end of the day it's all about finding new ways to generate awareness and leads. If you don't tap into your audience's visual side, then you are simply missing huge opportunities to connect.

Now that we've covered the importance of visual content, let's talk specifically about the reigning champ: the infographic. In the following chapter I will discuss how, what, and why infographics should be a part of every integrated marketing strategy.

1. http://techcrunch.com/2013/02/17/social-media-statistics-2012/
2. http://www.slideshare.net/LImarketingsolutions
3. http://blog.linkedin.com/2013/07/25/introducing-slideshares-new-infographics-player/
4. https://www.canva.com
5. https://www.haikudeck.com
6. http://prezi.com
7. http://www.columnfivemedia.com

in·fo·graph·ic
infō'grafik/
noun

A visual image such as a chart or diagram used to represent information or data.

CHAPTER 11

Twelve Insights for Achieving Visual Content Success with Infographics

Some marketing skeptics claim that infographics are dead. I disagree. I think *bad* infographics are dead, and always have been. Well-designed and executed infographics, on the other hand, are not just alive—they are a thriving and essential part of any integrated content marketing strategy[1]. And while we're on the subject, claiming that something is dead is so passé.

With all the competition for consumer attention on the web, it takes more than just creative wording to rivet eyeballs. An infographic is a compelling way to use visual content[2] to tell a rich story at a glance.

Here are some of the reasons why infographics are the perfect way to capture consumer attention:

- **Visual content is at an all-time high:** Social media sites that focus exclusively on images are swiftly gaining in popularity. Of course we know how successful Pinterest has become. And according to 2014 B2B Content Marketing Research, two of the top social media platforms that have experienced the biggest surges in use year over year are SlideShare (40% vs. 23%), and Instagram (22% vs. 7%).

- **Storytelling has gone visual:** As Ekaterina Walter points out in her fantastic book *The Power of Visual Storytelling*[3], "there is a need for our storytelling to become more visual. Our brains process visuals 60,000 times faster than text. And we decide in the split second whether we want to continue to consume more content from a company or brand based on how appealing the visuals are."

- **They put the "I" in image:** Of course, words are still the best way to communicate many types of information, but according to a 2011 study by Skyword, the total views of a piece of written content increase by 94%[4] when visual content, such as image or infographic, is embedded.

- **Competition improves quality:** The number of infographic vendors continues to grow, prompting lists of the best infographic design companies, such as this one[5] just published by *Visibility Magazine*.

- **Big data is big:** We have more access to data than ever before, and data is the very core of infographics.

Indeed, the competition to create an infographic that's viral-worthy is fierce, so you need a solid plan.

5 steps to creating killer infographics:

1. Come up with a concept to tell a timely story
2. Find or capture striking, reliable data to back it up
3. Design a visually winning infographic
4. Set clear marketing goals
5. Follow through on these goals with a marketing plan

That last step is one that harried marketers often treat as an afterthought or even skip, but without it, the other steps are pointless.

My experience (working at Marketo and LinkedIn) has shown me that a company's blog is the best permanent residence for an infographic. And it's a smart practice to offer an embed code on your blog for readers to easily grab so they can share the image elsewhere. Great infographics have wanderlust–they beg to travel and be consumed; that's why you can find them all over the web. So, the more seductive your infographic–and the more desirous companies, organizations, and individuals are to repost your infographic on their blogs and social media–the greater the chance of spreading your infographic and brand message quickly.

Why go through all this trouble for one piece of marketing content? The answer is four-fold:

4 benefits of a successful infographic

1. **It attracts attention:** An infographic is a visual interpretation of your brand message; a rich combination of words, data, and pictures in a fun format that can be easily shared.

2. **It has viral potential:** A viral piece of content is valuable–almost sacred to a brand. It's the Holy Grail of content from which consumers drink heavily. If you can get your infographic to go viral, you've won.

3. **It is fuel for your social and demand-gen programs:** An Infographic is easy to share on any medium, so its great content for social media sites, email marketing campaigns, and even in an eBook or on a printed brochure. It can be multi-purposed to the hilt.

4. **It attracts SEO linkbacks:** If influential people or companies link to your infographic from their websites and blogs, you get more than just a bigger audience–you also earn higher search engine rankings. Search engines consider an incoming link to your site from another reputable site proof positive that you are a bona fide content source.

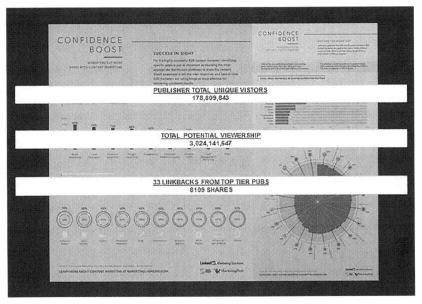

Figure 2: The first Infographic I Produced at LinkedIn and its Results

3 secret channels to showcase your infographic

Beyond your usual marketing channels, you can place your infographic in a few strategic places that many companies don't seem to take advantage of, which is inexplicable to me, since these channels are cheap-to-free and take very little effort. Here are my top three essential channels:

1. **SlideShare:** This presentation-sharing technology has been around for a while and is available to LinkedIn members to showcase their work visually within their profiles. A lot of LinkedIn members use SlideShare to display portfolios, for example. SlideShare recently upgraded its technology to host, display, and share infographics right from a company's profile page. Displaying your infographic on LinkedIn gives you insight into analytics and lead gen right from that page.

2. **Infographic directories:** Plenty of online directories allow you to display and then track traffic from your infographic back to your website or other call-to-action destinations. Search for your favorite using SearchRank's Quick List of Infographic Directories.[6]

3. **Press releases:** The days of hiring a publicist to issue a press release are long gone. Now, you can easily submit your release to online distribution services, such as PRWeb. Because many companies still distribute dry, text-only press releases, if your release includes creative and informative visual content front and center, news outlets are more likely to take notice and include it in their stories.

Infographics, when properly designed and executed, are popular marketing tools because they work. But they're not necessarily for every company, and aren't guaranteed to go viral, which is why a small faction of critics claim they aren't valuable marketing content. In my experience, whether an infographic is a huge hit or not, it's always a sound investment in your content marketing.

1. http://contentmarketinginstitute.com/developing-a-strategy
2. http://contentmarketinginstitute.com/2013/05/visual-content-auto-brands-help-audienc-es-get-picture
3. http://www.amazon.com/Power-Visual-Storytelling-Visuals-Videos-ebook/dp/B00HSO0XDK/ref=s-r_1_1?ie=UTF8&qid=1415839308&sr=8-1&keywords=Visual+Content+marketing
4. http://www.skyword.com/post/skyword-study-add-images-to-improve-content-performance/
5. http://www.visibilitymagazine.com/buyersguide/best_infographic_design_company
6. http://www.searchrank.com/blog/2011/11/quick-list-of-infographic-directoriesarchives.html

"WHERE'S YOUR WILL to be weird?"

—Jim Morrison

CHAPTER 12

Why You Should Give Your B2B Campaign to a B2C Agency

Recently Bryan Kramer[1] coined the term H2H (Human to Human) to replace the traditional B2B/B2C dichotomy. It struck a chord for marketers and gave them a simple mandate: Speak to people like they're people—not automatons. Get their attention with unexpected stories, headlines, and images. Gain their trust by speaking authoritatively, but in simple, quickly grok-able terms.

But what does it take to move a B2B brand into the H2H category? How do you break away from a predictable B2B marketing toolkit and reinvent your brand in more approachable, human terms? Try hiring a B2C agency. Here's why:

Simplify Your Message. Then Simplify it Again.

Modern marketers have all kinds of data and technology at their disposal. Social media and marketing automation platforms allow one-to-one conversations with almost infinite numbers of people. You can keep track of what you've said when, to whom, and how they responded. You may know where your target audience hangs out, what they're talking about, and maybe even what they're having for dinner.

But all that is for naught if you don't get this point: All those people you're talking to? They want supremely simple, straightforward answers to their questions.

Business decision-makers have complex problems to solve—problems that may require complex solutions. But a clear, uncomplicated answer grabs their attention every time. Good B2B marketers have known this for years, but B2C marketers have turned it into an art form.

That was the Big Idea behind *The Sophisticated Marketer's Guide*[2] that LinkedIn put together recently with the help of a boutique agency named Scorch out of St. Louis. Many LinkedIn users have a good understanding of social and content marketing, but they needed simple, straightforward answers to how they could make those approaches work on LinkedIn. *The Sophisticated Guide* breaks it down and gives them a great place to start.

Question Everything. No, Really.

A good B2C agency absolutely forces you to break the mold. The process might even make you a little uncomfortable. Sitting down with your new Creative Director could feel a bit like a visit to your shrink: "So … what do you think you 'know' about this audience, Joe?"

You may have to call off your company's brand police. You may feel as though you've fallen down a marketing rabbit hole. But if you can face those fears and stay focused, you just might come up with something that potential customers will sit up and pay attention to.

Remember that B2B Marketers Like to Have Fun Too

A B2C agency can add a certain element of entertainment to your content marketing and turn inspiration into content that drives revenue.

As an example, Marketo's The Big Marketing Activity Coloring Book came to life after The Smoking Gun posted the Foo Fighters' backstage rider. The genius that is Foo's frontman Dave Grohl doesn't just email a list of backstage demands to each venue; he created an illustrated storybook. That inspiration led to a fun-filled collaboration between me, Maria Pergolino, and the humans at Scorch. While it looks like "a giant piece of marketing chocolate cake," it's actually an incredibly influential piece of content. The point is that if I as a marketer were stuck in the classic B2B white paper mindset, one of the biggest pieces of viral content in Marketo's arsenal would have likely never happened.

Figure 3 The Big Markeing Activity Coloring Book[3]

Tell Absolutely Great Stories.

The occasionally traumatizing news for B2B is this: Connecting with decision makers in today's online marketplace is more about authenticity and relationships than it is about product benefits. Tell a great story, and you may just make that CIO late to his next meeting. Send him a list of product benefits and he'll save it to read later— if you're lucky.

But great stories are no simple thing. Compare, for example, this Microsoft video[4] to the "It's good to be a dad"[5] TV spot for Robinsons orange juice. The Robinsons spot leaves its most powerful moment for a plot twist at the end, showing the product only briefly. The Microsoft video starts with an emotionally powerful story about Sarah Churman, a deaf woman able to hear her children play for the first time. But it goes on to a long explanation of Microsoft's part in it all, topped off (in case you were wondering) by a quote from Sarah about how grateful she is–to Microsoft.

Don't get me wrong–Sarah's story is very sweet. It's compelling and I'm happy for her. But the Robinsons spot is pure genius, and Microsoft could learn a lot from it. Good storytellers understand the importance of leaving room for mystery. They know the difference between a story line that feels contrived and one that hits you in the gut and leaves you reeling with emotion. Those are the storytellers you'll find at a good B2C agency.

Using an agency focused on B2C clients opens up creative possibilities that the B2B world hasn't historically been open to. And that can help you break through your company's B2B mindset to access that common human language that Bryan Kramer talks about.

1. http://socialmediatoday.com/bryan-kramer/2115561/there-no-more-b2b-or-b2c-it-s-human-hu-man-h2h
2. http://marketing.linkedin.com/blog/introducing-the-sophisticated-marketers-guide-to-linkedin/
3. http://www.marketo.com/ebooks/the-big-marketing-activity-coloring-book/
4. https://www.youtube.com/watch?v=ikrsjFTfn1w
5. http://www.youtube.com/watch?v=RyeDBZaxFa8&feature=youtu.be

CHAPTER 13

Building a Content Marketing A-Team

Although the title of this chapter is a total cliché, I couldn't find a more clever way of describing this. In conversations with folks looking for content marketing advice, the question often asked of me is: "What does a world-class content marketing team look like?" The answer is much less complicated than you might think, and one based upon the last few years of a tremendous amount of trial and error.

Let me start by saying that if you are serious about content and don't have dedicated headcount or budget, you are likely going to be disappointed with your results and continue to miss opportunities. I'm not saying you need a Red Bull-sized budget, but you do need something in place. Once that is taken care of, the next step is to pull together the right team.

Here's how I think of the structure and process for a truly agile, cutting-edge content marketing machine for the modern marketer. I am not a fan of placing all of my eggs in one basket; I have found that agencies are usually great at one or two things so it's essential to mix it up.

Here's my formula for success:

1. **SEO Consultant/Agency (The Pilot)**—You absolutely need to lay the foundation for your content strategy based on SEO best practices and keyword research. Even though Hummingbird has made us less reliant on exact match keywords, these still play an important role in helping you determine the type of content to create and where you can make an impact.

2. **Creative Agency (The Faceman)**—Finding the right agency for conceptualizing, designing and repurposing (think Turkey Analogy)[1] your content is essential. Look for one that understands the "Big Rock" content strategy[2] and repurposing content for fueling social and demand-generation channels.

3. **Writers (The Muscle)**—I recommend working with two writers: One for eBook content, and one for high-level strategic guest posts. The eBook writer will work closely with the design agency mentioned above and the strategic writer will be key for creating guest posts that are geared towards a very specific audience.

4. **Visual Content Agency (Special Ops)**—When you need to present data in a visual manner, you need to bring in the big guns to make the biggest impact. Agencies that specialize in visual content can take data visualization to the next level. It's a very specific skill, but an essential part of any overall content marketing strategy moving forward.

5. **Content Marketing Manager (The Leader)**—And finally, you need someone who understands how all of these agencies and writers work together in order to fuel a full-on integrated marketing strategy. I call this the multi-dimensional modern marketer and they are quite in demand at the moment.

The leader of this content marketing band of misfits does not need to be an expert in any one of the areas mentioned above. But it is essential that they understand how all these moving parts can work together with the same goals in mind. And remember, this team doesn't have to cost a fortune, and doesn't have to be running full time in the background. As I mentioned in an earlier chapter, Content Marketing Expert Doug Kessler[3] says "aim for one home run per quarter." This was my focus and the exact formula I used to create The Sophisticated Marketer's Guide to LinkedIn[4] and what I will continue to use moving forward. I love it when a plan comes together.

This is how the process went when The Sophisticated Marketer's Guide was only an idea in my head:

1. Call with our SEO agency for keyword research around the topic/question to determine the competition and how quickly we might be able to make an impact. This research will also likely surface keywords and phrases that will help to build the case for creating the content as well as broadening the reach. It will also help with the language to use around messaging and targeting.

2. Call with our creative agency to talk about concept, scope and themes. I usually do a full brain dump of my idea, back it with the keyword research and then ask the agency to come back with three concepts that will be our starting point.

3. Call with the writer/editor. I recommend writing as much of this internally as possible, but this isn't always realistic. Start with a solid outline and then write as much as you can to fill in the content. A good outside writer/editor can flush out the rest by adding in stats, third-party quotes, etc. for reference and then do the final edits before publishing.

There are a tremendous number of marketing agencies out there, but some of them will try to sell you a $25,000 infographic. Unless that infographic comes with a free Airstream trailer, that's not a good deal at all. If you are in need of recommendations, connect with me on LinkedIn[5] and I am happy to share a few as I have worked with some amazing folks over the past few years.

1. http://marketing.linkedin.com/blog/leftover-turkey-a-content-marketers-dream/
2. http://fr.slideshare.net/Llmarketingsolutions/the-sophisticated-marketers-guide-to-linke-din-the-webinar
3. https://twitter.com/dougkessler
4. http://marketing.linkedin.com/blog/introducing-the-sophisticated-marketers-guide-to-linkedin/
5. https://www.linkedin.com/in/jsnmiller

"ALL I CAN Do is be me, Whoever that is."

– Bob Dylan

CHAPTER 14

How to Empower Employees as Content Champions

Do you have content writers on your staff? You probably do and don't even know it. Every one of your employees is a potential content creator and can be an important part of a successful content marketing strategy[1]. They were hired because of their expertise in a function that relates to your business and it's your job to help them get that domain expertise out of their heads and onto your blog. It might not be obvious to them that what they know about a particular function, industry or business practice might be valuable insight to your customers and prospects. It's your job as a marketer to encourage them to share their thoughts and expertise.

Break Down the Barriers to Writing

One of the most common barriers to getting your employees involved in content creation or contributing to the blog is the fear of writing a blog post. Those who have never done so before can be intimidated by putting their thoughts out into the world for all to see and comment upon. Start by telling them what's in it for them, e.g., it's good for their career/professional development, management recognition, etc.

One very useful resource that I have used to overcome this challenge is what I like to refer to as "the bible" of content marketing, *Content Rules* by Ann Handley and C.C. Chapman. This book is the essential guide for all content marketers, and includes some useful tools for getting new bloggers up and running. Ann and C.C. have put together a blogging template[2] that outlines the blogging process, making it easy for newbies to jump right in. Put that into place and then hold a few brown-bag lunch blog-training sessions at your office and you are primed for success.

Incentives Work Wonders

Now that you have the essential playbook (Content Rules) in hand and the helpful templates, it's time to incent participation. I recommend putting together a point system with tiered prizes for blog contribution. I've seen these types of incentive programs work wonders when coordinated by a smart content marketing manager. The following guidelines are based on Marketo's fantastic incentive program[3] for internal bloggers.

Level 1: For their first contribution, give bloggers something simple such as a branded t-shirt or Starbucks gift card. Even this type of reward can really get the ball rolling.

Level 2: For three blog posts, offer a more significant prize, such as a gift certificate to a fancy restaurant, tickets to a professional sports game, or a digital watch.

Level 3: For six blog posts, you can get even fancier, awarding iPods, noise-cancelling headphones, or other popular digital devices.

You can obviously take this program and its levels to any heights. But you will likely find that certain employees will find they enjoy contributing to the blog and may not need any incentive over time.

Don't Forget the Editorial Process

With all the new content entering your blogging pipeline, it's essential to have a quality check in place. A template will help out with any formatting issues, but remember, quality always trumps quantity in the world of content. You will need a final reviewer to check for grammar, add a bit of SEO optimization and add the post to your editorial calendar. (You do have an editorial calendar in place, right?)

Here are a couple of tools that I recommend for keeping a collaborative editorial calendar:

No budget—Google Docs works brilliantly

If you have budget—Curata, Kapost and Skyword are fantastic options for managing complex schedules and lots of moving parts

Ongoing Fuel for the Content Machine

Blogging programs such as these are vital to a successful content marketing strategy. Once momentum picks up, you will start seeing new ideas and topics along with fresh opinions and writing styles come out of the woodwork. It's an internal content awakening of sorts. But just as with any program, you'll need to give it TLC to keep it going strong.

Celebrate your contributors and call them out in a company newsletter after they get their first blog post published. Publish their blog contributions to your LinkedIn company page and run Sponsored Updates for the top performing posts. It's just another way to reward your internal content creators while making sure they know that their voice and expertise are contributing to the overall humanization of your brand online.

Your employees are the lifeblood of your business. Empowering them to contribute to such a powerful medium will likely deliver the most difficult kind of content to create: the organic kind.

---

1. http://business.linkedin.com/marketing-solutions/content-marketing/best-practices.html
2. http://www.contentrulesbook.com/extras/
3. http://www.blog.marketo.com/

Make Your interactions
with people transformational,
NOT just transactional.

—Patti Smith

CHAPTER 15

Is There Such a Thing as Having Too Much Content?

It's a question that comes up very often, so I thought I would pose it to a few experts to get their perspective.

I consulted with Ann Handley, Chief Content Officer of MarketingProfs; Joe Pulizzi, CMI's own Content Marketing Evangelist; C.C. Chapman, renowned storyteller, explorer, and humanitarian; Joe Chernov, VP of Marketing at HubSpot; and Marketo's own Co-Founder and VP Marketing, Jon Miller.

Here are some of their thoughts, as well as my own, based on our collective experience with best practices and processes for creating content.

Aim for epic

Ann Handley believes—and I agree—that quality always trumps quantity when it comes to content. "I don't think 'How much?' is the right question," she challenged. "It's more about how effective your content is. Focus on whether it's meeting your objectives: Is it igniting conversations? Is it enabling relationships? Is it sparking business?"

Producing information carelessly just to build your content library won't help your marketing efforts. In fact, that practice will only dilute your core points and distract your audience. Posting more thoughtful pieces less frequently is a strategic way to both control and spread your organization's brand message, while keeping your reputation as a thought leader going strong.

Content Marketing Institute's Joe Pulizzi also backed up this opinion in his recent post on the fallacy that more content is better: "Content volume is important. Enterprise organizations need lots of content in many different forms and multiple channels," he said. "But quality cannot be sacrificed. To break through the clutter, content must be epic."

Epic content marketing might seem like a daunting expectation, but if you aim for content that's original, imaginative, and sometimes even a little provocative, you're already halfway there. So, don't obsess over a content quota; instead, supply your audience with content that offers substance that they can't easily find elsewhere or produce on their own. (Like a blog that summarizes four different experts' opinions on a particular topic. You're welcome.)

Keep it short and compelling

In addition to focusing on the frequency of your posts, pay close attention to word count and significance. How long should each piece of content be, ideally? C.C. Chapman knows how to tell a riveting story, so I wanted his feedback on this content conundrum. "My philosophy is to follow the miniskirt approach: enough content to cover the essentials, but still keep it interesting," was his advice.

In other words, your content should include relevant and timely information that's concise. Don't drone on! People are busy, and their attention spans are short. Help them skim your content by grouping it with subtitles. Use callouts to focus their attention where it matters most. And instead of trying to say everything in one place, include links in your pieces to information that backs up your point. Linking to content from your own archives will keep your audience engaged with your marketing platform and bolster your credibility at the same time.

C.C. believes that there's an art to timing and keeping audiences engaged without ever boring them: "You need to produce constantly, because if you go silent, your audience might look elsewhere. And when that happens, it's hard to bring them back," he cautions. "If you are not creating and sharing information at least once a week on one of your channels, it's not enough."

It's all about being a "baller of balance," Marketo's VP of Marketing, Jon Miller asserts: "The challenge is maintaining a high bar of quality; if your content is not relevant and useful to your target personas—in other words, educational and entertaining—more content might actually hurt your efforts. Buyers are already overwhelmed by brands competing for their attention; don't make it worse with irrelevant content."

Measure what works

The marketer's job isn't only to produce content, but also to use analytics to identify the ideal volume and frequency. I asked Joe Chernov—who, by the way, was recently named as the Content Marketer of the Year—for his sage input on finding the right balance of quality and volume.

"The balance comes from the right amount of testing against what the overall objectives are," is what Joe told me. "The audience—not the publisher—determines content quality, and the same holds true for content volume. I've cut content output by 20% and I've still seen all KPIs increase because I [had been overproducing] the content."

I was thrilled to hear him mention testing, because it's such an important component of content marketing. With marketing automation tools, you can fine-tune your content output to what your audience engages with most, based on the metrics you see after each post.

Curata, using its own content marketing platform integrated with Marketo and Salesforce.com, completed an analysis of its blog posts.

The findings, as presented in the chart below, indicated that long form posts were generating many more leads than other types of posts. Insight from this analysis drove them to create more long form blog posts and fewer short form posts

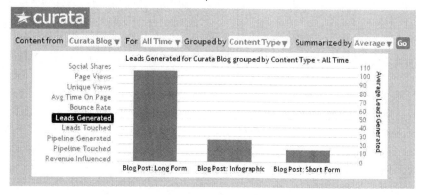

Like all marketing activities, your investment into content can exhibit diminishing returns. Doubling your investment might only return 40% greater results. But be realistic here. As Jon Miller says, "Most companies are at the low end of the content curve right now, so small incremental investments in additional content could yield large incremental returns."

"My advice," says Jon, "is to keep investing more while you move up the curve (perhaps taking funds from other marketing tactics—like trade shows—and moving them down the curve) until the marginal return of your incremental investment is at the same level as your other tactics."

Here's a quick visual to illustrate Jon's point:

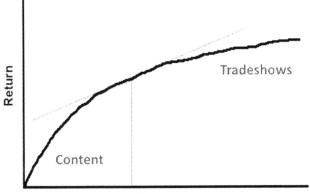

Doing more without investing additional resources? That sounds like the "right" amount of content for your budget to me. When you keep a close eye on metrics that pinpoint where your marketing efforts are on the curve, you'll know exactly where to optimize your marketing investment.

The content takeaway

It's important to have a regular cadence of content to "feed the machine." But the experts' consensus is that balance comes from focusing on quality over quantity, staying consistent and using tools to measure audience engagement. Once you find the perfect content rhythm for your blog, email marketing, and social channels, you just might discover that less content is bringing you more success.

CHAPTER 16

Your Content Kicks Butt, but is it Taking Names?

Superheroes are great role models, for children AND for marketers. They know their strengths, use them to their advantage and, at the end of the day, kick some serious butt. They also ensure they meet butt-kicking goals; the most effective superheroes take names—an inventory of butts kicked, if you will. Yes, that's their KPI.

So what KPI do content marketers use to determine if they are, indeed, kicking butt? According to IMN's 2013 *Content Marketing Survey Report*, the most prevalent KPI is lead generation. 44% of content marketers list "increased leads" as the primary goal of content marketing programs[1], up from 16% in 2012. This makes sense because for content marketing to be truly effective, it needs to have a positive impact on the bottom line.

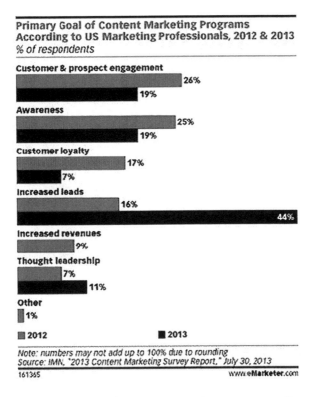

Primary Goal of Content Marketing Programs According to US Marketing Professionals, 2012 & 2013
% of respondents

Customer & prospect engagement
26%
19%

Awareness
25%
19%

Customer loyalty
17%
7%

Increased leads
16%
44%

Increased revenues
9%

Thought leadership
7%
11%

Other
1%

■ 2012   ■ 2013

Note: numbers may not add up to 100% due to rounding
Source: IMN, "2013 Content Marketing Survey Report," July 30, 2013
161365   www.eMarketer.com

If your content commands attention and stirs your audience to think or act a certain way, congratulations, you've got the "kicking butt" part of content marketing down. Now for the taking-names portion—here are four LinkedIn lead-generation tips to help you get a bigger return from your power-packing content.

Lead Generation Tip #1: Include a Compelling Call-to-Action That Proposes a Logical Next Step

Each click is an opportunity. When members of your target audience engage with your content then leave without taking an additional action, opportunity is lost.

What do you want your audience to do next? Do you want them to connect with you on social media? Do you want them to subscribe to your blog? Download a white paper? Request a demo?

Creating content with a goal in mind ensures you're not creating content just for the sake of creating it. Goal-oriented content puts a "why" behind each piece of content you create, and allows you to get better at guiding your audience to the next step.

To do this effectively, you need to map content to the appropriate buying stage. Consider the following fictional blog post titles:

The Novice's Guide to Marketing Automation

4 Things You Must Include In Your Marketing Automation RFP

Potential readers of each post will likely be at different stages of the buying cycle. For the second post, it might make sense to include a CTA for a competitive analysis report or a demo that leads to a lead-generation form. Readers of your "novice" post are less likely to fill out a lead-generation form at this point (unless you are offering a free piece of content or a tool that novices find desirable), however they may be interested in subscribing to your blog or following you on social channels.

Lead Generation Tip #2: Make Your Gated Content "Worth It"

Be careful here. On one hand, you want a headline and a teaser description that convinces your prospect to give up personal information in exchange for your content. If you're successful, you've got a new lead in the funnel. But what happens when your content doesn't live up to expectations?

According to a Content Marketing Institute and MarketingProfs 2012 report on B2B content marketing, less than half of all digital vendor content is found useful, and buyers feel that 22% of the buying process is wasted with ineffective content. Vendors who produce low-value content are 27% less likely to be considered an option, 40% less likely to win the sale. Your audience expects valuable content when they give up their personal information to get it. Don't let them down.

Lead Generation Tip #3: Use SlideShare

Not only is SlideShare super sharable and SEO-friendly, it's also a great way to generate leads. You can offer SlideShare viewers a teaser of your presentation and then gate the rest of your content with a lead-generation form. Give it a shot with your next SlideShare presentation and test lead-generation form placement within your presentation to see where it's most effective.

Lead Generation Tip #4: Always Be Testing

Optimization isn't just a marketing buzzword. It's how successful marketers ensure they are getting the best possible results.

Think about it this way: What would a one-percent conversion rate improvement mean for your company? For even a mid-market business, a one-percent uptick in new leads can mean millions of dollars in additional revenue. At the very least, you should test the big stuff (i.e., offers, headlines, major design elements and CTAs) and go from there. Of course, you'll want to adhere to some general do's and don'ts[2] when testing.

1. http://business.linkedin.com/marketing-solutions/content-marketing/best-practices.html
2. http://www.smashingmagazine.com/2010/06/24/the-ultimate-guide-to-a-b-testing/

CHAPTER 17
Three Simple Metrics

When it comes to measuring content marketing, how do you know if it's working? What measurements should you have in place?

I always like to mention the fact that I reported directly to Jon Miller, VP of Marketing at Marketo. While Jon is a marketer, he has a degree in Physics, so you can imagine how hellish it was for me to put together metrics that would matter to him and the CMO. It didn't help that Jon told me the ultimate metric he wanted me to focus on was to simply get people to like our company and what we do. How do you measure that?

Even with all the amazing technology available to marketers, there will always be an element of non-measurable outcomes in the world of inbound marketing. Moz.com's Rand Fishkin calls this "serendipitous marketing" and he presented a brilliant Whiteboard Friday[1] where he discusses the importance of investing time and resources here. Fishkin says, "Sticking to what can be easily measured often seems like the safest route, but avoiding the unknown also prevents some of the happier accidents from taking place."

That said, I still needed to report on the success of my inbound marketing campaigns and so that's where we leaned on three very simple metrics. There are hundreds of blogs out there suggesting hundreds of ways to measure your content marketing. I don't like to overcomplicate things. Just as I mentioned before that we need more relevant content, we need more relevant metrics.

Three Simple Metrics for Measuring Content Marketing Success

Here are the three that I feel lay the groundwork and ultimately prove the value of your content marketing efforts.

1. **Referral traffic.** You can measure this super easy, non-

complicated metric with Google Analytics. I suggest you focus on non-brand keyword referral traffic, which refers to people who are coming to your site without typing your brand name into the search engine. So what would have prompted them to visit your site? Well, it's very likely all that good content you're putting out there.

2. **Engagement.** I personally think it's only a matter of time before engagement plays a role in search engine rankings. The idea is if your content is encouraging engagement—people sharing it, liking it, plus-one-ing it—that is a sign of relevance. So the more engagement you get, the more relevant your content is. It's a good indicator of what is working and what you need to create more of. People will say, 'I only got five Tweets on this content.' Well was it the right five people? Because we don't necessarily need hundreds of thousands of shares; we need the right people engaging and sharing.

3. **Higher quality leads.** How quickly is your content accelerating the funnel or shortening the buying cycle? If your leads are coming in by way of your content and they are much closer to purchasing your product, that's a clear sign of success. This metric can be little bit tricky to measure depending on the sophistication of your marketing automation system. If you're not source-tracking each piece of content out there, then you're not going to be able to track success in this manner. Where did someone first engage with this piece of content? Was it the blog, an email drop, Facebook, LinkedIn, Twitter? You need to be able to track the engagement and leads being generated by every piece of your content.

---

1. http://moz.com/blog/investing-in-serendipitous-marketing-whiteboard-friday

"Performing is the easiest part of what I do, and Songwriting is the hardest."

— Neil Diamond

CHAPTER 18

Taking Your Content Global

6 Essential Tips for a Global Content Campaign Launch

One thing I've learned during my time as a content marketer is that it's a mistake to think about any content project in a silo. Just like you need to plan from the get-go to repurpose and reuse your eBook, presentation, white paper and other assets, you need to think about all the places your content will go. And when you're reaching out to a global audience, your content will be traveling far and wide. Yet according to the 2013 Global Content Marketing report from Cloudwords, over 60% of global marketers do not have a strategy for multilingual content marketing. That oversight leads to poor visibility into how much it will cost and how much time it will take to prepare content to go global. Here are six ways to make sure it doesn't get stuck at the borders.

1. **Planning, planning, planning, and a heads up.** Assuming your company is staffed by geographies, it's vital to let all of your "geos" know about the content initiative far in advance for planning purposes. Give your team a heads up with the idea and tentative timing for launch. Doing so as early as possible will give the geos a chance to put a placeholder into their demand-gen calendar and quarterly planning doc.

2. **It's all about the options.** Give your geos the option to localize the content themselves but strongly encourage them to use the same vendor that developed the original asset. In my experience, many geos prefer to translate and localize the content themselves, but this can quickly become complicated when additional vendors and stakeholders are added to an already delicate communication strategy. That's why it's best to push for one vendor to take each project as far as possible.

3. **Make sure the geos are involved as the project unfolds.** This means keeping them in the loop both with the concept and creative as it begins to take shape. Remember that although this piece is being created in one country, what works there doesn't necessarily translate over to the other seven or so that you are working with. By keeping a global vision in mind for the framework (for example, no country-specific imagery and non-global data points) it will be much easier to localize and translate the content.

4. **Get the source files.** Those geos that choose to localize and translate the content themselves will need the original source files from the vendor/agency. Getting these files can sometimes be a problem. For instance, your vendor/agency may charge you extra for these files—something you may not have planned for. Read the fine print on the statement of work and be sure that source files are part of the agreement.

5. **Determine which assets can be repurposed.** I have found that using the term "repurposed" isn't ideal when referring to the larger content initiative at hand, but it's fine to think this way

when it comes to the smaller elements. For example, can one blog post be translated easily to the different geos or easily updated for the launch? Can images be easily repurposed by simply updating the text for hero images (for your website homepage, resource center, blog feature etc.) banners, and social sharing?

6. **Measure individually but report collectively.** Of course it's important to set goals and success metrics for your global content initiatives. But reporting them individually can lead to a who-did-better sort of race. Keep in mind that this is a global campaign and the fact that you were able to create, coordinate, and execute alongside your fellow global marketing leads is the big story here. That means an individual reporting of success is going to be the secondary headline. Both should be celebrated, but at the end of the day we are all in this thing together.

CHAPTER 19

Thought Leadership: The What, the Why, and the How

These days, many people struggle when it comes to drawing the line between thought leadership and content marketing. I like how Jon Miller, VP of Marketing for Marketo, breaks it down:

"...both thought leadership and content marketing can very effectively build your awareness and brand, but...true thought leadership is much rarer. Thought leadership consists of ideas that require attention, that offer guidance or clarity and that can lead people in unexpected, sometimes contrarian directions (think of Seth Godin). Thought leadership needs to be educational and ideally provocative; content marketing can simply be fun or entertaining."

Three Types of Thought Leadership

There are three flavors of thought leadership: Industry, Product and Organizational. Here's more about each type, and how to select the optimal mix for your company.

Industry Thought Leadership

Standing out in your industry is the aim of many thought leadership programs. But what exactly does this mean and how do you achieve this goal?

At a minimum, it means you need to focus on the news, trends and forces shaping the market(s) you serve. Then you need to develop and share innovative thoughts and insights about those dynamics. Clearly spell out how your ideas surface newfound opportunities, provide an alternative path to success, or offer a novel approach to solving an entrenched problem that your audience is facing. Consider developing a contrarian point of view. After all, what's the value in hearing someone agree with what's happening in a particular industry? Don't just rehash what's being said—recalibrate people's thinking with a fresh perspective.

Product Thought Leadership

Once you've defined a new—and let's face it—best way for companies in a certain industry to go about business, you want to give them the means to get from point A to point B. Ideally your products (or services) are the vehicle for taking them down this better path. To help your audience understand how this vision can become reality, share best practices, strategic roadmaps, practical how-to's and other information that shows your product's potential for transformation. The content and ideas you share are the "evidence" of your thought leadership, and can inspire others to partner with your company.

Organizational Thought Leadership

Your thought leadership should reflect your company's vision, innovations and uniqueness. In other words, it should mirror your organization's culture. We could go a step further and say it should *drive* your company's culture. No matter how you look at it, your thought leadership and culture need to be in sync for your thought leadership to take wings.

What's the Best Mix for Us?

I recommend applying these different flavors of thought leadership based on what you can do well and where the opportunity lies. Commit to all three if you have the resources. That means you need to develop a point of view and produce a variety of content on industry, product and organization. But if your resources are limited, choose one and do it very well. For example, is there a gaping hole in your industry that you can fill? Maybe there's an opportunity for a quick win around culture and product, but high competition around industry. Bottom line: focus on the area(s) where you can make an impact and add value to the conversation instead of just adding noise.

Don't Stray from Your Core Strategy

As I said, it seems many B2B marketers have a hard time understanding where thought leadership ends and content marketing begins. In my mind, the two are intertwined. In fact, in numerous surveys, establishing thought leadership is often cited as one of the key reasons that B2B marketers engage in content marketing. No matter how you define or slice and dice thought leadership, it is always core to a company's communications strategy. And by injecting true thought leadership into your content, you can take it to new heights.

That said, it's important to grasp the interplay between your brand and corporate communications when it comes to thought leadership. When your organization establishes itself as a thought leader, your brand gets polished to a new gleam. That's because your brand stands for the promise you make to your prospects, customers, shareholders and any other vested parties.

At the same time, thought leadership that sets you apart can help your organization stay top of mind as B2B buyers make their way through a sometimes lengthy purchase process. As buyers digest–and connect with–your thoughts and ideas, they begin trusting you as a reliable source and brand. And that means your company is much more likely to make the short list of contenders. In fact, Corporate Visions found that 74% of buyers choose the company that was FIRST to add value as they are defining their buying vision.

Aligning Thought Leadership with Messaging Strategy

So how do you go about getting into thought leadership?

Effective thought leaders map their topics to key themes that intersect with their target audience's pressing concerns and what their organization can do to help address those concerns. Put another way, they make sure there's consistency in the company's mission and vision, what the company delivers in the market, and its marketing messages.

At the same time, it's important to align thought leadership efforts with your company's overall strategic goals so you can drive a meaningful outcome from the program.

There are No Shortcuts on the Road to Thought Leadership

While any person or company can establish itself as a thought leader, it doesn't happen overnight. It takes a strategy and commitment over the long term. In fact, the ultimate value of being a thought leader is that you're seen as a reliable and credible source of strategic thinking. And that can serve you for many years. But you need to build a plan to reach that goal.

Just don't think you have to go it alone. Here's a handy checklist for thought leadership success:

- Define what thought leadership means to you/your organization
- Secure top-level buy-in and support
- Align thought leadership with product/service and organizational leadership goals
- Establish a process for brainstorming, vetting and developing a manageable number of ideas
- Develop a unique and groundbreaking viewpoint
- Use content marketing concepts and best practices to disseminate your thought leadership
- Deliver thought leadership at every stage of the buying cycle
- Define success criteria and measure and report on it
- Commit to a long-term initiative/program

Why It's Important to Measure Thought Leadership

All marketers know they're expected to prove the value they're delivering. The same holds true when it comes to thought leadership—you need to define your goals and then measure and report on them. To start, outline what you expect from your thought leadership program.

ITSMA (Information Technology Services Marketing Association) breaks thought leadership influence into three categories:

- **Reputation.** Arguably a key goal of establishing thought leadership is cultivating a reputation as a trusted authority. Ideally this reputation will prompt others to solicit your input and thoughts on strategic issues and take this into account as they form their own opinions and make strategic decisions.

- **Relationships.** Thought leadership can be your inroads to developing important connections with other recognized authorities, industry leaders and potential customers, partners and more.

- **Revenue.** Ultimately, you'd like to see that your thought leadership initiative helps you generate more sales.

You will likely deliver your thought leadership via the same channels you use to deliver other company and marketing messages—including written content and speaking engagements. That means you can use the same measurements to determine the reach and impact of your efforts, such as number of:

- Content downloads and views
- Event (in person and online) registrants and attendees
- Comments on blog posts
- Mentions in respected and relevant publications
- Retweets and new followers on social media channels
- Top-level search results for ideas you're putting forth

But take this a step further and tie your thought leadership activities to more strategic and meaningful outcomes, such as number of:

- Executive-level meetings scheduled
- Analyst meetings secured
- Invitations to participate on advisory boards

CHAPTER 20

3 Ways PR and Content Can Work Together

"We must start distinguishing good and bad content and helping brands improve their content long before it is pitched. This means that we, as PR pros, must become proficient at recognizing bad data, bad analysis of data, lack of creativity, rewrites and plagiarism, and myriad other symptoms that define bad content marketing." —Chris Penn, SHIFT Communications

In March 2014, Nielsen released a report claiming that branded content is not all it's cracked up to be. The results of their study paint a poor picture for the performance of content marketing by brands and new trends such as native advertising. It was strange for me to see PR folks take the results and run with this as a "victory" over content marketers. In my opinion, that's the wrong attitude.

While the study was certainly interesting, what it fails to point out is that there are simply not a ton of companies doing branded content well. It's an ongoing process as brands learn to talk less about themselves and more about how they can be helpful. It's a movement towards branded content that is so good that you are proud to put your company name on it. Or better yet, as Jay Baer famously said, "Marketing so good your customers will pay for it."

I remember seeing the same kind of backlash around using social media marketing for B2B. There were reports coming out the wazoo claiming that social does not work for B2B, but the problem was simply that no one was doing it well. Fast-forward a year or two and there are a tremendous number of B2B companies using social to drive brand awareness and generate leads. The same could be said in this case as a lot of companies out there are still refining their branded content strategy.

Instead of pitting PR vs Content, here are three ways they can, and should be, working together.

1. **Rally 'Round the Infographic**–The traditional press release has undergone several makeovers in recent years and forward-thinking companies are now embracing what I call the hybrid press release. This new press release incorporates rich media including infographics and videos to help take the story to a whole new level with reporters and influencers alike. Creating a hybrid press release is done by breaking down the silos of PR, Content and Social and rolling them into one cross-functional team. One of my favorite examples is the process of including an infographic in your press release. It's created by the content team, promoted by the social team, and launched by the PR team. The orchestration is a beautiful thing, and the end result will very likely make a much bigger impact than anything one of these teams could achieve by going it alone. Not too mention all three will share the success as opposed to the tendency towards sibling rivalry in marketing.

2. **Share Contacts**–There is so much overlap between influencers, analysts, reporters, and thought leaders that it doesn't make sense to keep these folks segregated on different teams. I recommend building a master list of everyone, showing columns for email address, Twitter handle, expertise (inbound, social, sales etc.), and who has the best relationship for outreach. This is perfect for developing a hybrid PR launch that includes all the appropriate people for outreach in support of a specific campaign or initiative. This doc can also serve as a checklist of sorts for keeping track of who has been briefed or contacted around each campaign.

3. **Generate a Unified Monthly Report**–Sure, you can send a list of PR links per campaign to your CMO. But what if you sent over a full report that included the coverage, along with a list of the thought leaders, reporters, influencers, analysts, and others who shared, Tweeted, Liked, mentioned or simply was touched by your combined efforts? You can take it a step further by pulling together a list of Twitter handles, media sites and influencer blogs and tracking them in a product such as Radian6. That way

you can see if your Share of Voice and Share of Conversation increase, or pinpoint a spike in mentions based on your combined outreach efforts.

BONUS TIP: Score Your Influencer Engagement

One of my favorite ways to track the success of a unified PR, Content, and Social team is to create what I call the "Influencer Score Card." Pull together a list of influencers to target from analysts, reporters, thought leaders, etc., and score them visually from green to red on engagement. For example, your three columns could be:

1. Mentioned you in social

2. Wrote about your brand/company

3. Had a face-to-face meeting

These will all start as red (not engaged) but over the course of your campaign they should move to yellow (getting warmer/in process) and ultimately green (engaged). It may not be pretty in the beginning, but if you are successful, you will be able to quickly show the fruits of your efforts with an easy-to-interpret visual that should be much more green than red.

The Influencer Scorecard Example

Influencer	Mentions/Shares	F2F meeting	Linkbacks	Score
	🟢	🔴	🟢	⚪
	🟢	🟢	🟢	🟢

🟢 Green　🔴 Red　⚪ Yellow

A tremendous shift is happening in the content world that will affect both PR folks and Content Marketers. It's best to get aligned now so that we can all work towards that coveted fully integrated strategy that is the future of marketing.

CHAPTER 21

Real-Time Content Marketing

Real-time marketing and engagement

When we think of real-time marketing, the term newsjacking comes up quite often. I love the concept of newsjacking, but in order to take advantage of it you need a dedicated writer who can shift focus from your own content to something newsjack-worthy at the drop of a dime. I just don't believe that it's a realistic strategy for many marketers because it leads us from telling our own stories to chasing other people's stories.

But there are elements of real-time marketing that I think should be a part of every content marketing strategy. And if you plan accordingly, it shouldn't take up too much time and effort.

I think of real-time marketing in three ways:

- Waiting for the moment
- In the moment
- Anticipating the moment

Content that is waiting for the moment has been created for a purpose while also living to see another day—sort of an ever-growing content repository. Perhaps you put this content into a resource section on your website as sort of a library, organized by topic and searchable. This can easily be repurposed or used in campaigns when the time is right.

Content that is in the moment is similar to newsjacking. A really great example of real-time marketing is, of course, the legendary dunk in the dark Oreo Super Bowl ad[1] that quickly became the go-to example. Now we can't all have a creative agency working on Sundays at a moment's notice, but it's certainly a brilliant example to reference.

One of my favorite examples of content in the moment comes from Smart Car. They saw a Tweet by this guy who was walking in Boston or NY and [Tweeted], "I just saw a bird crap on a Smart Car. Totaled it." In response, Smart Car created an infographic based on how much bird crap it would take to actually demolish a Smart Car, and they Tweeted it back to him. That's a pretty expensive reply, but after *Mashable* picked it up, *Huffington Post* and everybody else started talking about it. The story generated some amazing brand awareness. It humanized the company.

The third type of real-time marketing is what I call anticipating the moment, which is where we're moving with predictive analytics. It's the ability to produce relevant content based on data from previous interactions. I think Amazon does a great job with that. It reminds me of the movie *Minority Report*, where the pre-cogs see the future and the cops act on it. I think content that anticipates the moment is really the most exciting type and it's going to be interesting to see how technology continues to evolve so marketers can take advantage of it.

1. http://www.huffingtonpost.com/2013/02/04/oreos-super-bowl-tweet-dunk-dark_n_2615333.html

Ego is the GREAT Enemy. Ego will hold you back every Single time.

−Nikki Sixx

CHAPTER 22

Is Your Ego Hijacking Your Content?

There's a lot of talk about "mindfulness" these days. Everyone from corporate leaders to Washington politicos[1] is touting the benefits of meditation and mindful awareness on health, stress levels, and the bottom line. Even Silicon Valley visionaries[2] are looking for ways to detach themselves from the onslaught of interruptions they themselves helped create.

As content marketers, it can be hard to know what to make of this reality. How do we reconcile our audiences' need to unplug and find a meaningful daily focus with our own drive to generate a buzz of comments, Likes, shares, plus ones, and Retweets? Were we better off when those social signals were not around to serve as a barometer for our content?

The answer may be as simple as this question: how much of that buzz is actually coming from specific prospects? Is your content helping people and leading to actual sales? If not, you may benefit from a little centering yourself. Take a deep breath, and let's focus on letting go of some egocentric habits that could be getting in the way.

1. Content Marketing: The Ultimate Anti-Selfie

The idea that sometimes it's good to step aside and listen to your audience, rather than persist in wowing them with your personal brilliance, is as old as marketing itself. But social media has made listening mandatory.

When you create content, it should reflect the composition of the community you're trying to reach. You are the snapshot-taker, not the subject. That way, your content has a chance of contributing to your audience's conversations, solving its concerns, and getting noticed. As Lauren Vargas at Aetna[3] has said, "Go beyond the ego search." Don't just look for what people are saying about your company. Look at topics people are congregating around, and figure out how you can make a difference in the conversation.

2. Forget Personal Opinion. What Do the Numbers Say?

Marketing 2.0 is a numbers game. If you're not testing your assumptions, testing new channels, and studying the metrics available to you at each stage of the sales funnel[4], you're missing opportunities. Yes, you may have years of marketing experience and a good feel for what works and what doesn't. But, to hack your way to the top of your industry, you need a broader, more objective viewpoint.

Here's a simple example: headlines. They're all-important—everyone knows that. But even the most experienced content writers can't always tell the difference between a good headline and one that will go viral. So what do you do? Run a quick A/B test. Find a clear winner. Then launch. Your writers will thank you if you share the results with them, so they can be growth hackers, too.

3. Be Willing to Tolerate Discomfort.

No one likes sleeping out in the cold, but let's face it—sometimes that's the only way you get to the top of the mountain. Dave Kerpen[5] has a great post about starting his first business with his wife. In it, he talks about how difficult it was, how they risked their very relationship and had trouble meeting payroll, getting loans, and managing cash flow. It's not a pretty story, but it's an authentic one. Authenticity, as he says later[6], "breeds trust, and trust breeds business."

People can tell immediately when you're afraid to confront a really tough topic, but they invariably become inspired and engaged when they see that you're taking a risk, showing them something they haven't seen before, or tackling a nearly unsolvable problem. To succeed, you have to let go of the outcome your ego is fixated on and trust that you'll be able to handle whatever happens next.

4. Tell a Story That's Bigger Than You.

Ann Handley said it perfectly in her post about Chipotle's "Scarecrow" video[7]: "Your story is not about you; it's what you do for others." When you go beyond the sale to offer content that makes a difference for the world as a whole, you have a good chance of striking a chord that will resonate with current and potential customers for a good long while.

Are you telling a story that will still be inspiring long after you've left the blogosphere, long after the trend of which it speaks is ancient history? If so, you may be getting somewhere.

5. Let Your Content Live! Don't Let Fear Steal Its Thunder.

Sometimes letting go of ego actually frees you to promote yourself. Think about the last time you gave a presentation to your boss or stood up to speak in front of an audience. Sometimes you have to just exude confidence even when you feel completely uncertain of yourself, right?

The same goes for putting your content out there. After you've done your best, gotten input from your team, and produced a great blog post, video, or SlideShare…let it live! Post it in places your target audience will see it, make sure you've targeted appropriately, and by all means, put some paid promotion behind it. That way, you extend your content's life beyond your immediate circle of friends and followers. You have nothing to lose but that sense of feeling safely and solidly unknown in the world. And that, my friend, is another form of ego.

1. http://www.huffingtonpost.com/2013/07/25/tim-ryan-quiet-time-caucus_n_3653247.html
2. http://www.linkedin.com/today/post/article/20131114080217-32720-silicon-val-ley-trends-nov-2013?trk=vsrp_influencer_content_res_name&trkInfo=VSRPsear-chId%3A53948611389922489805%2CVSRPtargetId%3A5806660009047633920%2CVSRPc-mpt%3Aprimary
3. http://www.socialmediaexaminer.com/how-aetna-is-building-a-social-media-presence/
4. http://contentmarketinginstitute.com/2013/11/build-scorecard-measure-content-marketing/
5. http://www.linkedin.com/today/post/article/20130131135544-15077789-thank-you-small-busi-ness?trk=mp-reader-card
6. https://www.linkedin.com/pulse/article/20130912085641-15077789-7-simple-rules-for-amazing-content-marketing
7. https://www.linkedin.com/pulse/article/20130915181453-6474349-the-biggest-marketing-lesson-from-chipotle-s-scarecrow-video-and-it-s-not-to-start-with-a-billion-dollars-and-fiona-apple

SIDE 2: SOCIAL

Welcome to Side 2. There are a few classic albums where the flip side is just as important as the first. Just as Led Zeppelin IV kicks off side one with the all-time classic "Black Dog" and concludes with the epic "Stairway to Heaven," side 2 is not far behind with "Misty Mountain Hop" and "When the Levee Breaks." That's what I had in mind when structuring this book. While the subject of content is truly the heart and soul of this book, social media marketing continues the story and equally compliments what preceded it.

Social media marketing is hard and it takes time and patience in order to begin seeing results. It's essential that your business has a social presence; if it does not you are simply missing opportunities. More importantly, you need to have a strategy and specific tactics in place in order to achieve set goals. Goals should be modest at first and then dialed up to become more aggressive as you begin to find your social groove. As you start to integrate social into your overall marketing strategy, it's important to not only run social media campaigns, but to start thinking about how you can make all of your marketing campaigns truly social. What campaigns do you already have in place that could benefit from a social lift?

CHAPTER 23

Your Philosophical Approach to Social is Killin' Me

There's a time and place for philosophy when it comes to marketing, but the world of social media has been focused on this for way too long.

Buzzwords and clichés such as engagement, transparency, authenticity and *there's no ROI to measure from social* are giving us forward-thinking marketers a bad name. It's time to move from a philosophical approach and get to some metrics that matter.

Philosophy cannot compete with the science of marketing.

I consider philosophy to be a method that develops arguments based on reason rather than observation or experience.

The social media "Socrates" is how I like to refer to the folks who are notorious for asking questions but not answering, claiming to lack wisdom concerning the subjects about which they question others.

While philosophical musings serve a purpose, in the golden age of social media, these teachings have exceeded their usefulness. Marketers being measured on their contributions need to focus on concrete tactics. That's why ***it's time to enter the age of enlightened metrics and results.***

The ROI of Social is No Longer a Mystery

There is no mystery around the ROI of social. We know what it looks like and how to measure for it. The problem is that there are many more folks complaining about social ROI instead of actually doing something about it.

At the end of the day it's all about tracking how social impacts prospect and customer movement through the buying cycle. This goes beyond top of funnel to cover the entire buying journey, including the post-sales stage.

Social can play a major role in accelerating the buying cycle, driving revenue, and encouraging customer loyalty. **But you must have the technology in place to measure its impact.** That technology is marketing automation, and it's powered by good content and a smart marketing team.

Automation is a Good Thing

Before you get on your soapbox to say, "There has to be a human involved," let me reply with, **of course there does.**

I am not talking about automated social media responses; I am talking about integrating your social with a marketing automation platform. Doing so is essential when leads are coming in straight from the social-sphere.

These early-stage, top-of-funnel leads are almost never ready to buy. That's why it's vital to have a nurture strategy in place to guide these buyers along the path to purchase and revenues.

If you are only dealing with a few leads at a time, this is manageable using ad hoc, manual methods. But if you want to scale, you are going to need some help. And it's worth it to get that help in the form of marketing automation. Setting up nurturing tracks for social leads will automate and personalize the delivery of the next piece of content based on the buyer's digital body language both inside and outside of social. And more relevant content leads to better engagement.

Social Media Does Work for B2B

It's all about tracking.

Some draw a line in the sand when it comes to the ways that B2C and B2B marketers can benefit through social marketing. Many still believe that only B2C brands should—and can effectively—engage their target audience via social media. But B2B marketers who use marketing automation to deliver relevant content and track their social campaigns by lead source are proving them wrong. They know that some leads originate from social and others are influenced by social. As customers and buyers continue using social to research products and services, these channels are going to play an increasingly important role.

Specifically, these channels will drive more business for companies. And B2B brands will be able to directly measure the results. Marketers can identify a lead that makes it into the pipeline and turns into closed revenue directly from a social network. They can also see which social channels and campaigns are accelerating movement through the funnel, shortening the sales cycle and ultimately driving additional revenue.

By the way, during my time at Marketo, I found several instances of revenue won as a direct result of our presence and engagement on Twitter, Facebook and LinkedIn, so *pay attention to all of them equally.* I have seen revenue won on six figure deals from a first touch in social, and I think it's going to become much more frequent moving forward.

When all is said and done, it's the social media doers that are in the trenches day in and day out who will lead this charge. It's a new world for B2B marketers, and one that will likely differentiate your company from the competition and ultimately drive more business.

"I'd prefer 1,000 followers, friends, and fans that actually meant Something, rather than 10 million that weren't engaged."

—Jared Leto

CHAPTER 24

Debunking the "Vanity Metrics"

In December 2012, Harvard Business Review published a post titled "Why Your Social Media Metrics Are a Waste of Time,"[1] in which the author referred to social media metrics as "false idols of analytics." While she made a few valid points, her unfavorable blanket statement really fired me up because it negates the true potential that social media offers when it comes to driving revenue.

Let's start at what I believe to be the root of the problem. Social media metrics used to be referred to as "vanity metrics" because they were shrouded in mystery when it came to tying them to anything useful, especially revenue generation. Those days are over. Marketers can now connect the dots to prove how social engagement leads to new revenues. That's why social media metrics are now as vital for companies to closely monitor as the hard-core revenue metrics. So, with all due respect to the author, if she doesn't understand how these channels can contribute to a company's sales pipeline—and help ultimately cross-sell and up-sell current customers—her statement is groundless.

Some organizations, including perhaps the author's, are seeing lackluster social media results because they simply don't know what to measure and can't tie social back to pipeline or revenue. Or perhaps it's that they don't invest the necessary time and don't engage correctly in social channels. Either way, that's what I call the lazy marketer syndrome.

Anyone involved with social as a sales and marketing channel knows that social is not a magical solution to driving more sales. But, as we've learned from case studies and a ton of trial and error, social is a fantastic addition to almost any overall marketing strategy. And it will only become more important as the world's best marketers continue to move towards more fully integrated marketing campaigns.

So don't listen to those who say social isn't effective for lead generation, sales acceleration, and driving revenue. Chances are, these naysayers are turned off because they've failed miserably at executing social and/or they've discovered that it simply didn't work for their product or service. Sure, failure is possible, but I see brands enjoying success through social with some of the most boring products in the world. That's when I think that those who blame social for their own failures just don't want to admit that they prefer to focus their efforts elsewhere.

Metrics for the C-Suites, and Metrics for the Rest of Us

In addition to making a grossly unfair sweeping statement, the author also briefly defined "four of the most important metrics you can follow": relevant revenue, sales volume, customer retention and relevant growth. She then asked readers to "notice how little they have to do with popular social media metrics." She claimed that to measure the value of your social media activities "you have to look at the results the company is getting overall and track how social media was involved in moving the needle." Doing that, she believes, is how you'll find "the only relevant social media metrics."

What? The only relevant social media metrics? For whom? Everyone? Not quite.

This argument is best addressed with the captain-of-the-ship analogy. The captain of the ship (your CXOs) only cares about two things: where the ship is heading and how you get there. But down in the ship's boiler room are the practitioners (marketing teams) with a laundry list of important things that have to happen in order for any charter to be successful. This is where you as a marketer must ask the right questions to determine how social is affecting the course of the ship.

Here are questions that you should actively seek to answer in order to provide "relevant" social media metrics.

1. How do I know what type of content most interests my customers or prospects?

2. How many people are discussing problems that my product or service can help solve?

3. How do I get my content in front of these folks when they are doing their research?

4. How is my content performing?

5. Is anyone talking about my company, brand or product?

6. Are they saying good or bad things? (Let's not forget the power of peer to peer when it comes to social)

7. How many people are recommending my product or service?

8. How do I know if my social channels are referring quality leads?

9. How are these social touch points affecting my sales cycles?

Those of us who analyze social media know that it's time-consuming. So it's no real surprise that when busy marketers don't see immediate results, they often write social off and give up on proving its value. But that needs to change because it's essential that you know which social channels your audience uses and how to reach and engage them there.

The best marketers today maintain two sets of metrics:

1. One for determining overall strategy by providing customer and prospect insights to guide your content marketing strategy and messaging.

2. The hard-core sales and revenue metrics that your CXOs love, which track social as a lead source and as touch points across the sales funnel.

At the end of the day, you need to be measuring both.

Depending on how sophisticated your marketing software is, I recommend tracking social by lead source and using a multi-touch attribution model so that you can see how social is impacting your sales funnel through increased lead quality, pipeline, and ultimately revenue won. With the right software in place, you can even forecast the future contribution of social channels.

At Marketo, we knew the exact impact of social metrics on our core topics and tied back many of our campaigns to precise ROI. In addition, we viewed social engagement across the sales funnel and buying cycle to determine the real impact of social on our overall marketing strategy. If we could do all that, so can you.

1. http://blogs.hbr.org/cs/2012/12/why_your_social_media_metrics.html

"Being a RockStar is the intersection of who you are and who you want to be."

—Slash

CHAPTER 25

The Six Golden Rules of Social Media Marketing

Social media has found a solid place in just about every company's marketing plans and with good reason. Just consider these findings from the 2013 State of Inbound Marketing report put out by HubSpot:

- 52% of all marketers found a customer via Facebook in 2013
- 43% of all marketers found a customer via LinkedIn in 2013
- 36% of all marketers found a customer via Twitter in 2013

We all know it can be tough to keep up with the constantly evolving world of social. But as social media continues to dominate B2B marketing discussions and becomes an essential part of any solid marketing strategy, it's worthwhile to revisit the fundamentals. Here's a quick refresher of what I consider to be the six golden rules of social media marketing.

Heed this advice, and you'll always have a solid foundation for your social media marketing.

1. **Don't take yourself too seriously.** It should be obvious, but social media is about being social, and that means you need a good personality to make your brand likable. It's great to have serious content with serious messaging, but it's also okay to have fun and entertain with your content on occasion. With this in mind, carefully consider who you select to represent your brand on social media—obviously someone who is socially awkward or uptight in social situations is not the right choice.

2. **Social as an inbound tactic is not enough.** Regardless of tactic, it's rare that any single marketing approach or program is going to deliver the desired results—especially in a world where your target audience is finding and interacting with you via multiple channels. This is true of social as an inbound marketing tactic; for your business to benefit fully from social, you should combine it with outbound marketing. And don't think by outbound marketing I'm talking strictly non-promotional. Never underestimate what a bit of paid promotion can do to extend the reach of your organic messaging.

3. **Start with good content, solid offers, and a clear call to action.** Without well-produced, engaging content featuring a clear call to action, any and all tactics you employ will most likely fail. This tried-and-true trio of power is just as important in social media as it is anywhere else. Make sure your content is relevant and motivates the audience to take action, and be clear about what you want your audience to do after consuming your content or engaging with your brand.

4. **Always add value.** At the end of the day, if you are not providing some sort of value to your prospects and customers, you are not doing your job. Here is an easy test: put yourself in your prospects' shoes and ask if what you are offering is of any value—from their perspective. If not, kill it and start over. Trial and error is the key.

5. **Never forget that social is a two-way street.** No one likes being talked at. Yes, broadcast your message, but remember to keep the lines of communication open in both directions. When contacted, always respond quickly and sincerely. Be sure to mix up your messaging and use a combination of helpful and sometime entertaining content and offers. And stay away from formal, business speak—try to keep things conversational.

6. **The 4-1-1 Rule:** This idea from Content Marketing Institute[1] founder Joe Pulizzi[2] and Tippingpoint Labs is based on Twitter engagement, but can and should be modified and applied to each and every social media channel. The rule states that for every one self-serving Tweet, you should Retweet one relevant Tweet and, most importantly, share four pieces of relevant content written by others. The basic idea here is to share more non-promotional posts before you go in for a soft or hard sell. It's also about not pretending that you or your company has all the answers—it's a good social practice to share the spotlight with others.

1. http://www.junta42.com/
2. https://twitter.com/juntajoe

CHAPTER 26

The Truth about Social Media Leads

The Truth about Social Media Leads

There are hundreds of differing opinions regarding the effectiveness of using social media for lead generation[1]. This is my opinion and it comes from over two years of trial and error using what I consider to be the best tools available for the social media marketer.

Encouraging top-of-funnel engagement

Social is an essential channel for the modern marketer. Just consider that the 2013 State of Digital Marketing report published by Webmarketing123[2] found that social media drove revenue for one-third of B2C companies and one-fifth of B2B organizations. According to Mark Yolton, senior vice president of digital, social and communities at SAP[3], "Social media marketing is no longer a nice to have—it's a must have. Our customers expect it. Our competitors are all doing it. And unless we embrace and excel at social media marketing integrated into the full marketing mix, we'll be at a competitive disadvantage."

Inbound is not enough

Inbound alone is not your answer; it's part of the equation for success. Combining inbound and outbound can multiply the number of views you generate, dramatically increase sharing, and ultimately increase the number of potential customers who see your content. At Marketo, we called this the Inbound Marketing Multiplier.

I cannot stress this point enough: using inbound alone to generate leads with social media is like hanging out with only the same group of friends from elementary school your entire life. Adding a bit of paid promotion (i.e., outbound marketing) is the only way to tap into the power of peer to peer. In other words, it's how you break through to the coveted friends of friends, or second-degree connections, while targeting social users and growing your overall reach.

Consider the example of Marketo using social campaigns to promote its gated content. It uses a variety of channels to make existing prospects and customers aware of its newest content. But in the process, it hopes to reach future customers. For example, when Marketo released an eBook about email, it researched email marketing experts on Twitter and then targeted those people's followers with a Tweet directing them to a landing page to download the eBook[4].

Whether you take advantage of LinkedIn Ads[5], Promoted Tweets, or Facebook Ads, social advertising can get your content seen by a much larger audience. Just remember to tailor your content for each channel. Get familiar with the best practices for each social channel so you can maximize engagement.

Social media leads must be nurtured

Social plays a key role throughout your entire sales pipeline. This includes the time before you even identify prospects (while they research and follow your thought leadership on social media sites). And it extends to the time after they become buyers (as they remain loyal customers through retention and cross- and up-sell efforts).

But social *leads* are often not ready to buy so you need to nurture them properly. Throwing thousands of unqualified leads into your funnel every month is a complete waste of time if they are never going to buy your product. The solution is to target appropriately and keep your content strategy focused on the pain points and hot topics of interest to your target personas. Content fuels social for sure, but having too much content that is way too broad can be a waste of resources.

If a lead falls into a funnel and no one is around...

What good is putting all of this into practice if you cannot track your success and determine if these leads are turning into customers? Make sure you are using a platform such as marketing automation to track lead source[6]. I prefer to track each social channel individually so that I can tell which one is most effective. Then, I break down the cost per lead and compare it to other sources.

In a nutshell

So there you have it. The truth around social media leads straight and to the point. The bottom line is that social needs to be integrated across your entire marketing strategy in order to be effective. It's also not going to be free as it requires staff and a budget, but that's for another chapter. Of course there are some details I skipped over here, but I invite you to download the Definitive Guide to Social Marketing[7] for a full lesson.

1. http://www.marketo.com/small-medium-business/social-marketing.php
2. http://marketingland.com/social-media-driving-revenue-for-one-third-of-b2c-companies-one-fifth-of-b2b-firms-report-64256
3. http://www.emarketer.com/Article/How-B2Bs-Working-Social-Leads/1010162#sthash.Q4Z82DGp.dpuf
4. http://www.slideshare.net/hootsuite/case-studymarketo-32413372
5. https://www.linkedin.com/ads/
6. http://www.marketo.com/
7. http://www.marketo.com/definitive-guides/social-marketing/

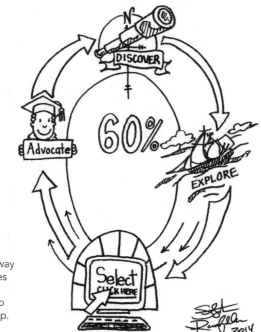

Figure 1 Buyers are 60% of the way through the sales process before they are ready to talk to a sales rep.

CHAPTER 27

A Crash Course in Social Selling

Social Selling is one of the current buzzwords that you absolutely need to pay attention to. It's the way forward for the modern day digital salesperson that is looking to exceed their quota and become a sales linchpin within their organization. Funny enough, it's a hell of a lot like influencer marketing so chances are you are already doing it. The next step is how to get your sales folks to do the same. Since LinkedIn is the best place to get the most value from social selling, that's where I will be focusing this chapter. So without further ado, here are my top real-world tips for sales professionals to build relationships and close more deals using social selling.

While it's not a numbers game necessarily, it is a networking game.

The winners will be those who are connecting with decision makers that they are looking to do business with and gain insights about them and their behavior. In this current world where relationships are the new currency, the sales folks with the best networks will become rock stars.

The Aberdeen Group defines social selling as the utilization of one of three techniques, which includes:

- **Social Collaboration**—sharing information internally or with partners to pool knowledge on how to generate more leads and sales

- **External Listening**—gathering and interpreting information or content produced by clients and prospects

- **External Participation**—providing prospects with relevant and helpful content or information to build relationships and positively impact future buying decisions

The Aberdeen Group provides further compelling evidence as to the benefits of using social selling.

- 73% of salespeople who used social selling techniques met or exceeded their quota.

- Sales teams that use social selling techniques exceed their quota 31% more than non-users.

- 57% of top performers have closed a deal that was originated through social media.

So how can a sales professional best utilize LinkedIn for social selling? It really boils down to three things: building your network on LinkedIn, identifying your prospects, and then engaging with them.

10 Ways that Best-in-Class sales teams are using bleeding-edge Social Selling techniques to be more productive on LinkedIn

1. **Lay the foundation with a solid company page**—Once you begin the process of implementing a Social Selling strategy, it's vital to have a "home base" on LinkedIn for your messaging, content, products/services, and campaigns. Encourage current customers to follow your page and post helpful targeted content consistently. When you need that extra push, try using a Sponsored Update to reach beyond your initial following.

2. **The "Who's viewed your profile" play**—I love how the "Funnelholic" and Social Selling expert Craig Rosenberg uses this technique. He says, "On LinkedIn, the prospect clicks on YOU. You aren't "nameless salesguy x calling me again"—they looked at your profile. It's a prime opportunity to talk to them. Isn't that better than "checking in"? They see your face, glance at your headline and summary… It is especially effective with people you have already connected with. (Think lead nurturing)."

3. **Using InMail for personalized email messaging**—Matt Heinz from Heinz Marketing recommends "taking three minutes to learn three things about someone before reaching out to them" and I absolutely agree. Leverage the insights you can gather from profiles and other social networks to indicate that you've done research on the person you're connecting with. For example, reference a blog post you've read by that person, or a presentation you viewed.

4. **Organize your prospecting with LinkedIn contacts**—With LinkedIn Contacts you can bring together your address books, emails and calendars, and keep them up to date in one central place. LinkedIn will automatically pull in the details of your past conversations and meetings, and bring those details directly into your prospect's profile. You can take it a step further by utilizing Tags, Notes and Reminder features as well.

5. **Leverage the power of LinkedIn Groups**—Not only are LinkedIn Groups a great way to build a personal brand, but if you're a member of the same group as another user, you can message them as if they are a first-degree connection. In addition, group members are also able to view the profiles of other members of the same group without being connected.

6. **Give your LinkedIn updates wings**—Say you post an update to LinkedIn that you'd like to share with your Twitter followers as well. With the check of a box you can easily syndicate that update to Twitter by selecting the Public + Twitter option in the Share With dropdown before clicking Share in the LinkedIn update composer.

7. **Leverage @mentions in your status updates**—In 2013, LinkedIn rolled out the ability to tag or @mention other users and companies in status updates—much like the way it works on Facebook and Twitter. Want another LinkedIn user or company to see your status update? Include the @ symbol immediately followed by the user's/company's name in your status update. As a result, that user/company will get alerted that you mentioned them, and their name will also link to their profile/page in the status update itself.

8. **4-1-1 Rule**—As I mentioned earlier, the 4-1-1 Rule was coined by Tippingpoint Labs and Joe Pulizzi of the Content Marketing Institute. Again, the rule states:

   "For every one self-serving Tweet, you should Retweet one relevant Tweet and, most importantly, share four pieces of relevant content written by others."

   Apply this simple rule to the activity on your Personal Profile and your LinkedIn Company Page, and you're golden. For social selling, the 4-1-1 Rule is particularly useful when applied to building relationships with prospective customers. Developing this kind of trust hinges on your ability to foster an informative dialogue regularly—and sharing all that content can help you do just that. It also keeps you at the front of prospects' minds as they move through the buying phase.

9. **Get your employees in on the discussion**—LinkedIn isn't just for marketing and sales folks; in fact it provides everyone in your organization with a path to become a thought leader and establish their personal brand. Consider third-party apps like GaggleAMP and Addvocate to empower employees to share your company's most important content with their networks.

10. **Take a cue from the marketing team**—Reach out to the folks on your social, content and PR teams as they are likely seasoned pros at posting great content and engaging within social. For example, there are many parallels between Social Selling and influencer/customer marketing. Your colleagues can likely give you some tips around the messaging and content that resonates with your target audience, which you can then apply specifically to your prospects.

CHAPTER 28

A Crash Course in Native Advertising

In the US last year, more than $4.6 billion was spent on social media advertising, 35% of which was for social native ads. It is predicted that by 2017, this figure will increase to nearly $11 billion, with social native advertising comprising 58% of spend. If Native Advertising is not part of your marketing strategy moving forward, then you will simply be missing opportunities. This is one of the most important chapters in this book and a vital lesson for social media and content marketers alike, so pay attention to what follows.

What is Native Advertising?

According to Copyblogger's 2014 status report[1], 49% of respondents don't know what native advertising is and 24% are hardly familiar with it. This is a troublesome stat but one that I think will quickly be updated as the modern marketer discovers the multi-benefits of adding native ads into their approach to a fully integrated marketing strategy.

One could argue that the first signs of native advertising emerged with the search engines. For example, when people search on Google, ads can appear at the top of the page, on the side of the page, or on the bottom of the page. These ads appear above the organic results, in the native environment of the user experience, hence the term Native Advertising.

At its core, native advertising is about how brands now work with

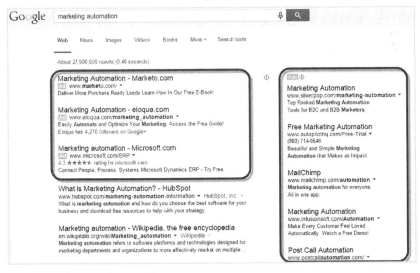

Figure 2 Early signs of native advertising

social networks and online publications to reach their target audience. It's advertising that doesn't look like advertising because it's an ad in the user's native environment.

Native advertising's influence on a broad range of media, including mobile and social advertising, will allow marketers and agencies to justify and continue to invest in native budgets for the foreseeable future.

Business Insider[2] defines native advertising in the context of social media as:

Ads that are seamlessly integrated into a user's feed and are nearly indistinguishable from organic content.

In other words, it's simply attempting to gain attention by providing content in the context of the user's experience.

So what are examples of native advertising?

- A promoted Tweet on Twitter
- Suggested post on Facebook
- Sponsored update on LinkedIn
- A video that plays before you read an NPR article
- A full-page ad between Flipboard pages

So how does this differ from display ads online–the square MPU units, leaderboards that straddle the top of pages and several other industry-standard formats? Native ads are in the flow of editorial content.

The Value of Delivering In-Context Ads

Native advertising is about more than just matching the look and feel of the site; you also need to match the nature of the content. Successful native ads provide high-quality content in a way that is seamless to the end user. And it's working. According to research from IPG media Lab and Sharethrough[3], native ads are viewed for the same amount of time as editorial content and are much more likely to be shared than a banner ad (32% versus 19% of respondents who said they would share a display ad).

Native advertising is especially useful at the top of funnel: a practice of using content to build trust and engagement with would-be customers. When a publication such as BuzzFeed works with a brand like Virgin Mobile, it isn't just to create great native content that its loyal readers see–it is with a view to the content going viral and being seen all over the web. Display advertising could never be used to accomplish that goal–at least not at a cost that most companies can afford. After all, each time a banner is served, there is an incremental cost to the advertiser. The same isn't true for native advertising.

Whether a revenue stream for a social network or as a complement to an online publisher's content stream, native ads answer a criticism that may yet pop much of the current content marketing bubble: "How does it scale?"

Native Ads and Mobile

With the increasing popularity of smartphones, more people are using their mobile devices than their desktops to check their social accounts. And social networks are responsible for at least 17% of all the time consumers spend on mobile devices.

Why is this so important to marketers? Because these ads look, feel, and work fluidly across mobile and PC platforms and are viewed within a user's social media stream, and that helps brands build effective campaigns across all devices.

When we look at LinkedIn specifically, we find that 38% of unique visiting members come through mobile apps and weekly mobile page views for LinkedIn have jumped 250% year-over-year. In fact 70% of the clicks from LinkedIn's Sponsored Updates come from mobile. Smart marketers are taking advantage of this shift by increasing their spend on mobile marketing, and integrating their ads seamlessly into the social feeds of their target audiences with native advertising.

The infographic below provides an in-depth look at the rise of mobile and native advertising and offers predictions for the future.

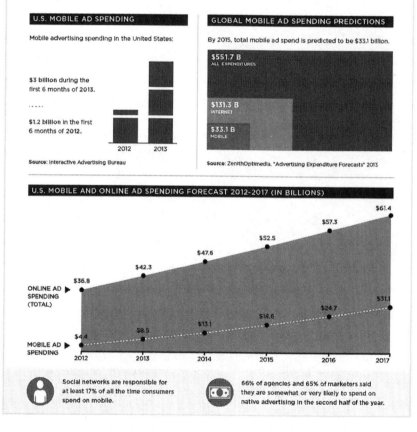

IN THE SOCIAL STREAM
FILTERING THROUGH MOBILE AND NATIVE ADS

Mobile and native advertising are gaining increasing popularity. With more social media users checking their accounts via mobile devices than on their computers, in-stream, mobile ads are quickly becoming advertisers' chosen method for getting their message front and center. On mobile's smaller screens, it's the user experience that counts the most.

THE RISE OF MOBILE AND NATIVE ADS

By combining mobile and social advertising, in-stream native ads are created. These ads look, feel, and work fluidly across mobile and PC platforms and are viewed within a user's social media stream, which helps brands build effective campaigns for all devices.

U.S. MOBILE AD SPENDING

Mobile advertising spending in the United States:

$3 billion during the first 6 months of 2013.

$1.2 billion in the first 6 months of 2012.

2012   2013

Source: Interactive Advertising Bureau

GLOBAL MOBILE AD SPENDING PREDICTIONS

By 2015, total mobile ad spend is predicted to be $33.1 billion.

$551.7 B ALL EXPENDITURES

$131.3 B INTERNET

$33.1 B MOBILE

Source: ZenithOptimedia, "Advertising Expenditure Forecasts" 2013

U.S. MOBILE AND ONLINE AD SPENDING FORECAST 2012-2017 (IN BILLIONS)

ONLINE AD SPENDING (TOTAL)
$36.8 $42.3 $47.6 $52.5 $57.3 $61.4

MOBILE AD SPENDING
$4.4 $8.5 $13.1 $18.6 $24.7 $33.1

2012   2013   2014   2015   2016   2017

Social networks are responsible for at least 17% of all the time consumers spend on mobile.

66% of agencies and 65% of marketers said they are somewhat or very likely to spend on native advertising in the second half of the year.

Figure 3 Source: http://www.slideshare.net/LImarketingsolutions/the-riseofnativeand-mobileadsinfographic

All the Ways Businesses Benefit from Native Advertising

Native advertising goes hand in hand with content marketing–after all, the idea is to share relevant, useful information. Perhaps content marketing thought leader Joe Pulizzi explains it best[4]: "Sponsored content and advertorials have been around for a long time. The difference today is that native advertising is truly a part of the content stream, like what we see in Facebook, Twitter or LinkedIn advertising. What I like about this for small businesses is that this can be a great rent-to-own strategy. If you haven't built an engaged audience yet, you have to get your content out there in a way that will ultimately build an audience."

So what options are available to you when it comes to native advertising? Here are a few examples:

- In-Feed Placements
- Paid Search Units
- Recommendation Widgets
- Promoted Listings

Check out the IAB playbook[5] for a complete breakdown of the six types of native advertising and guidance on choosing the best option for your needs. Regardless of which option you choose, this is what I believe native advertising is great at achieving:

- Brand awareness
- Lead generation
- Event registration
- Expanding thought leadership

The last point is one that should catch the attention of PR professionals. Some in PR worry that native advertising could potentially replace "the pitch." While that might be true, it promises to do so in the best way possible. With the targeting capabilities offered by native ads, it's much easier to get your content in front of your target audience, as well as the targeted press/media accounts. If you can't get the media to cover your story, do an end run by targeting the audience of that media with native ads. In this way, native advertising becomes a powerful PR tool–

one that will pick up the slack as press releases continue to lose their effectiveness.

Here are two native-ad types available to you via the major social media networks:

On LinkedIn, Direct Sponsored Content lets you personalize and test content in the newsfeed *without* first creating posts on your LinkedIn Company Page. And because you can send personalized messages to specific audiences, you can test and retest a variety of content in real time until you get it right. In other words, you can conduct A/B tests across audience segments and optimize content for specific audiences.

Similarly, on Facebook, you can publish a 'dark post' or Unpublished Page Post. What this means is that you can use newsfeed style ads without publishing them to your page's newsfeed but with full control over who sees what message.

Direct Sponsored Content on LinkedIn and Unpublished Page Posts on Facebook allow you to:

- A/B test your messaging/headlines
- Personalize the content (such as by location or job title)
- Control the content that goes on your page

1. http://www.copyblogger.com/native-advertising-2014/
2. http://www.businessinsider.com/the-rise-of-social-native-advertising-2013-10#ixzz2pMa2VkHx
3. http://www.sharethrough.com/2013/05/infographic-native-advertising-effective-ness-study-by-ipg-media-labs/
4. http://www.linkedin.com/in/joepulizzi
5. http://www.iab.net/media/file/IAB-Native-Advertising-Playbook2.pdf

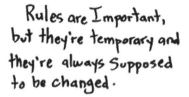

Rules are Important,
but they're temporary and
they're always supposed
to be changed.

-John Lydon

CHAPTER 29

Building a Kick-Ass Social Media Dashboard

If you are tasked with building a social media dashboard to track your efforts, look no further than this chapter. I have built many dashboards over the years and as a personal resolution to making my job easier, I decided to cut to the chase and get to the metrics that matter most. That means cutting out the everyday metrics that litter and cloud up the social media manager's real success story.

Now I am not saying that tracking followers, fans, sentiment, etc. is not important, but those are the vanity metrics that tend to give social media a bad name. Those metrics are great leading indicators but they don't really tie back to your business' bottom line: driving revenue.

A good place to start is by establishing baselines early and focusing on the social metrics that can really move the needle for your business. You are going to need a few tools for this one. If you are serious about measuring your social media program, then it's going to take some budget. I prefer to use a combination of the Salesforce Marketing Cloud (Radian6), Google Analytics, and a marketing automation platform.

I suggest building a simple dashboard to track and update these metrics on a weekly or monthly basis. You can then monitor trends and set goals for growth based on what's working. If your metrics are not moving in the right direction or seem to be stalled, try mixing up your messaging and experimenting with different posting times and frequency.

Here are six metrics that I have found to be highly effective in determining social media success that I recommend measuring on a weekly/monthly basis.

1. **Referring Traffic from Social (Google Analytics)**–Google Analytics is a fantastic way to measure how much traffic is being referred to your website from the various social channels. Set up goals based on the actions you want your visitors to complete such as creating a free trial or filling out a form. Boosting your social efforts should bring more traffic to your website.

2. **Conversions from Social (Google Analytics)**–This one is pretty self-explanatory. Set up conversions or goals, as Google Analytics likes to call them, and simply measure the source of your conversions. Is the referral traffic coming from social converting? If not, then adjust your content strategy as your content may not be referring folks who match your buyer profile.

3. **Share of Voice (Marketing Cloud)**–In social media, Share of Voice (SOV) refers to the number of conversations about your company vs. those about your competitors/market. The value of online customer and prospect interaction can be tied to the share of voice metric, which I like to call "The Big Picture Show." The formula for calculating SOV is simple: divide the number of conversations or mentions of your brand by the total number of conversations or mentions about other brands in your

market. Segment brand mentions by social channel to uncover opportunities for improvement. You may find that your efforts in one particular channel are going unnoticed, but excelling in another.

Share of Voice = Your Mentions / (Total Mentions for Competitive Companies/Brands)

4. **Share of Conversation (Salesforce Marketing Cloud)**–Very similar to the Share of Voice metric but instead of total mentions of your brand vs. for your competitors, this focuses more on specific topical conversations. For example when I was at Marketo, it was very useful to understand how much of the marketing automation conversations taking place online were mentioning Marketo.

5. **Sentiment (Salesforce Marketing Cloud)**–Sentiment analysis can be thought of as opinion mining. Although it is an imperfect science, often ignoring the human element of sarcasm or simple context, it's still very useful as a measure of success. To be completely accurate, you need to track this manually. Go through your mentions and tag them as positive, neutral or negative. Add up the totals and measure over time. Are the good mentions growing and the negative mentions decreasing?

6. **Pipeline Contribution (Marketing Automation)**–This is a very interesting metric. Once you define what a meaningful social goal is for your business (e.g., share, form fill out, Like, Tweet, etc.), you can track each of those goals through the marketing funnel. Then by looking at a multi-touch attribution model, you can determine how these social touches contributed to pipeline creation.

The world of social media ROI is still evolving and there will of course be some trial and error involved when putting your measurement strategy together. Stick with it and you're likely to develop a powerful new source of revenue that in many cases costs a lot less than traditional media. Over time you will begin to see correlations between social media and growth in your organization's revenue, website traffic, and overall buzz.

CHAPTER 30

The Importance of Keeping Your Cool in the World of Social Media

Navigating the world of social media can be like making your way through the Wild West. In a split second you can find yourself receiving a virtual high five and then immediately be involved in a shootout at the O.K. Corral. This is both the beauty and the beast of social media. It can be a marketer's best friend or worst enemy depending on your ability to keep your cool.

Welcome to the Jungle

As a social media marketer you will absolutely be tested. Frustrated customers, envious and jealous competitors, everyday Woody Woodpecker-like troublemakers, and more are running amok. Social marketing allows people to publicly vent their frustrations—and while there is absolutely nothing wrong with that, whether those rants become a problem or an opportunity all depends on how you respond.

It happens every single day across the board. Businesses and marketers seem to fly off the handle when challenged in the social realm. Consider this horrific account[1] of a business owner who seems to have completely lost his mind verbally attacking a customer over a complaint. It eventually escalated into one of the most-read stories of the day and a true PR nightmare for what looks to be a pretty decent restaurant.

You will be called out, you will be challenged, you will be hurt, offended, and quite frankly pissed off. Remember, there will always be people trying to poke holes in your opinions or strategies. You can't please everyone all the time, and you shouldn't be trying to in the first place. But handle these situations well, and you will be rewarded.

The important thing to remember is to keep your cool. As much as you would like to roar back with your own righteous opinion, it's not the answer. If it's an angry customer you are engaging, simply try your best to understand their issue and offer help. I would also suggest engaging your customer support or product team when someone seems particularly heated, letting the wider audience know that you take this seriously and you want the best possible outcome for the customer. You can often turn a hater or critic into an advocate by taking this approach.

How to Handle Rage Against the Social Marketing Machine

You may also find yourself the target of "hate mail" from those you're trying to reach by running ads in and around social media platforms. It's probably only a matter of time before you are the email recipient of the classic message "Dear so and so, get out of my newsfeed."

I am a huge advocate of social advertising and I get that there are folks out there who are annoyed by seeing ads in their different streams, but let's remember that these are free services. Facebook and Twitter need to make money in order to improve the user experience and this is how they do so.

Even though it's a different situation from the one described above, this is the time—once again—to be a smart, calm marketer. Reply when necessary and ignore, delete, and move on from the ones that don't warrant a response. To address someone who is upset because one of your ads appeared in their newsfeed, simply let them know how they can opt out. They have made it very clear that they are not your target audience so there is no need to try to convince them of the value of hearing from you.

Social ads are continually evolving. As the targeting gets better on both Twitter and Facebook and other channels, I believe we are going to see these ads and sponsored posts become less intrusive, more relevant, and actually helpful in many cases. The better my social networks can understand my behavior and throw me an ad or two that can solve a problem, recommend a gift, or remind me about an upcoming event, the more open I am to seeing those ads.

The Haters Eventually Get Their Comeuppance

If it's a competitor taking jabs or calling you out, no matter how nasty, take a deep breath, step back and respond when necessary but take the high road when you can.

If you are constantly taking low blows and potshots from your competitors, then you must be doing something right. In this day and age, it's vital to pay attention to what your competitors are up to. But acting like a vulture circling a corpse and waiting to pick them apart is another thing altogether. And anyone who adopts this negative stance will get theirs in due time.

Competitors who constantly take shots at you in the world of social are digging their own grave. Most of the folks who see these jabs have more than likely already chosen a side, but those who haven't are the ones with the power. The competitors who are talking more about your product or service instead of paying attention to their own simply reek of desperation. In some cases it can make the entire industry look bad.

Wear a Thick Skin and Focus on the Good

For those who choose to fight back, take a deep breath, put yourself in the other person's shoes, and respond as you would want to be responded to. You will likely be able to determine within a few back-and-forths whether or not the issue at hand can be resolved or if it's a lost cause. If it's the latter, move on to the next. Getting into a shoving match in an open forum does nothing for either party involved. But staying helpful and positive even when someone is on the attack can pay off over and over again. When others in the community see that you have made an attempt to help, you've essentially won the match and will likely be safe from future attacks. Even if you face a stubborn critic, naysayer or what have you, as community members see you trying to do the right thing, they will often chime in to show support for your efforts. And that goes a long way to giving you a good name in the Wild West of social media.

The key takeaway here? Don't take things personally. The importance of having thick skin in and around social media is only going to become more important as more and more voices add their two cents and seek validation from an online audience. Celebrate what you do well, reach out to every person who says something nice about your business and reward them with a simple thank you.

1. http://boston.eater.com/archives/2012/11/28/pigalle-to-customer-you-must-enjoy-vomit-you-btch.php

SIDE 3: ALL TOGETHER NOW

"Some People tap their feet, Some People Snap their fingers, and Some People Sway back and forth. I Just Sorta do 'em all together, I guess."

– Elvis Presley

CHAPTER 31

How to Hire a Rockstar to Do All of This

Finding and hiring a marketing rockstar who can manage your content and social efforts is going to be challenging. This is currently one of the most sought after positions in the space, especially in the world of B2B marketing. The first thing I would recommend doing is to craft a compelling job description, tap your current network, and get the word out. You may not be able to find a "rockstar" who has the necessary experience you are looking for, but keep in mind that you may need to find someone with potential and then empower them to become a marketing rockstar. Someone took a chance on me early on in my career and that provided the platform and fuel, while I provided the ambition.

I have hired quite a few content marketers over the years and I can tell you that the most important attribute that I look for is their ability to write. If they are a good writer and know how to craft a story, the rest of this stuff can all be learned. With that being said, here are twelve questions that I ask during the interview process with all candidates who will be focused on content marketing. While there are not right or wrong answers specifically to the questions below, the answers will paint a very good picture of who the candidate is.

12 Questions to Ask When Hiring a Content Marketing Manager

1. What do you think is the most important skill needed to become a successful content marketer?

2. What would be the first piece of content you would create?

3. In your opinion, what's more important: paid, owned, or earned media?

4. Give me an example of an integrated marketing campaign and how you collaborated with other departments.

5. How would you define your personal brand and how do you cultivate it?

6. What's your Klout score? (Just kidding, I would never hire someone based on this alone)

7. What's more important: strategy or execution? (Force them to pick one)

8. Best examples of content marketing? Who do you think is doing it well? (B2B and B2C)

9. Where do you get your inspiration for content pieces or stories?

10. How do you measure the impact of your writing and whether or not it is effective?

11. What do you predict will be the biggest trend in content marketing in the next 12 months?

12. Who do you consider the most important influencers for your content, should you get this position?

Then give them some homework. At LinkedIn we ask our potential candidates to create a simple SlideShare presentation around content marketing. It's a free tool to use and hopefully they are already using SlideShare as a content channel. It doesn't have to be designed amazingly well, but there are lots of ways to get creative here and stand out from the pack.

One last point I want to make here. It's a question that comes up a lot whenever I speak at events. The question of, "Why would I want to invest in creating a marketing rockstar or thought leader only to have them build up a following and take it with them someday?" The answer is simple. This will happen whether or not you would like it to. The personal brand will come along for the ride and certainly follow a marketer wherever he or she may go to next. The important thing to do is to ask yourself, "Do I have the environment to build the next thought leader in the space?" Smart marketers who are looking for opportunities need to know that they have the opportunity to build their personal brand and thought leadership with whichever company they decide to join. As a hiring manager you need to make it known that your company supports this.

CHAPTER 32

What KISS Can Teach You about Building a Modern Marketing Team (How to Organize Your Team for Success)

It should be no surprise to anyone who knows me how big of a KISS fan I am. While traveling back from seeing their 40th anniversary tour, I started thinking about how great these guys have been as far as building the ultimate marketing machine. The more I thought about it, the more similarities I found between Paul and Gene's approach to the band, and how it can describe the perfectly optimized modern marketing team.

Let me explain. As I have illustrated in the image above, you can see

KISS in all their glory identified as if they were a marketing team inside of a company. Why this makes sense to me:

The four unique band members work together to deliver an amazing product. In this case, kick-ass rock 'n' roll music. The same can be said for your marketing organization. It's vital to break down the silos that SEO, social, content, and demand gen currently sit in across many organizations and have them all sit together, collaborating effectively. Why is this? SEO lays the groundwork, while social fuels content, and content fuels demand gen.

They consistently deliver content that their fans want to consume and share. I'm talking about albums here of course, as KISS has delivered what I would call "Big Rock" content in the form of records on a regular basis throughout their entire career.

Their PR efforts guide their vision as the hottest band in the world. PR is the fifth member of the band. Doc McGhee is the band's Publicist/Manager and he does a fantastic job working very closely with the band to guide their communication efforts to the world. There's a current trend in the content marketing space where PR folks are fighting branded content instead of embracing it. There is a HUGE opportunity for the entire marketing team and PR to be working together much more effectively. (Refer back to Chapter 20.)

They deliver amazing experiences on tour. Event marketing is a huge part of the demand-gen process, and in order to be successful, content, social, PR, demand gen and SEO all need to be working together. Just as KISS delivers an amazing experience for their "customers and prospects" (lifelong fans along with a new generation of fans) marketing teams should take a cue from KISS and pull together to deliver exceptional marketing events as part of their overall integrated strategy.

They built a thriving community. KISS has built an incredibly dedicated community of fans and advocates globally known as the KISS Army. I am a card-carrying member and proud to be one. Just as with any community-building effort, this takes time. Marketers who don't take the time to build a community that will consume and share their own good content will likely not succeed. Now I'm not saying you need a community the size of the KISS Army, but I am saying that you need a community that is big enough to support your content efforts. Take a cue from KISS by giving your communities the attention they deserve and make them feel a part of something special, a movement if you will.

KISS figured this out years ago and I think marketers can benefit from a similar mindset. From my experience over the past few years, this is what a perfectly optimized marketing machine will look like moving forward.

"Try just a little bit of
tenderness, that's all you
got to do."

— Otis Redding

CHAPTER 33

Stop Hating on the Automation, Try a Little Tenderness

There's a preconceived notion among some in the B2B world that marketing automation is a bad idea, right up there with pop-under ads. This misconception likely stems from the early days of social media marketing, when desperate, unscrupulous companies used automated third-party services to blast what amounted to spam across their social channels 24/7. While that sort of automation is terrible, maybe even downright unforgivable, the last thing you want to do is discount automation altogether. Don't be a hater; there's so much here for a marketer to love.

But don't take my word for it, have a look at the latest stats around marketing automation and its implications:

41% of B2B Marketers plan to increase their marketing automation budget in 2014. (Source: PepperGlobal)[1]

63% of companies that are outgrowing their competitors use marketing automation software. (Source: Position2)[2]

Gartner estimates a **15% savings on creative production** when businesses use a marketing automation system. (Source: Gartner via HubSpot)[3]

78% of high-performing marketers say that marketing automation software is responsible for improving revenue contribution. (Source: Position2)[4]

Even though I cringe whenever I hear a so-called expert preach that "all marketing automation is bad," I don't take it personally. It's all about education, and I'm always happy to talk to people about the future-forward technologies propelling today's marketing automation software tools[5]. So, in this chapter, I'm going to baby step your doubting mind to the concept of embracing automation in marketing. Because the crazy paradox about automation is that, when done right, it can actually empower you to get up close and personal with your audience.

Automate the Mundane and Focus on the Dynamic

Marketing automation platforms allow you to automate the mundane and pain-in-the-ass tasks needed to scale online marketing efforts. Before the engagement purists jump all over me, I want to make it clear that you'll still need a good human team creating that content. You'll never be able to replace the creativity of your writers and graphic designers with robots. But by planning marketing messages ahead of time, you can focus on active, in-the-moment marketing tasks. Imagine freeing marketers so that they have more time to actually market! When marketers are able to focus on being proactive in their jobs, prospects and customers are guaranteed a better experience.

Personalize the Experience Precisely

Aside from automating the most routine tasks, there are things you can do with marketing automation that you can't do manually. Your customers don't want to be talked at; they want to be talked to in a way that makes them feel like you're listening to their unique needs. But having one-to-one conversations with hundreds, thousands, or even tens of thousands of people is pretty much impossible when handled manually. With marketing automation platforms, you can create customized conversations that scale to the masses.

Ironically, automation can be the driving force behind—not a killer of—truly personalized experiences for your customers and prospects. While a prospect is on your website researching your products, you can use marketing automation tools to dynamically present just the right content to him in his preferred channel and at the perfect time. The result is the singular goal of marketing: buyers and customers perceive that your brand is perfectly in tune with their needs.

Scale, Measure, and Drive

At the end of the day marketing automation is here to scale, measure, and drive revenue. While that doesn't sound as sexy as social, content, and SEO, it is certainly an essential component of the overall integrated marketing strategy. It also explains why the topic of marketing ROI has been gaining so much traction across the digital marketing space.

Perhaps the most valuable aspect of marketing automation is that you can use it to better measure your campaign results quickly and easily, and then make adjustments on the fly. While marketing stats were once hidden behind veils that prevented us from measuring campaign effectiveness—forcing marketers to hazard guesses about what was actually working—those veils have been lifted by sophisticated metrics tools. We can now precisely measure the effectiveness of our social, email, and other types of marketing campaigns, as well as the true ROI they deliver.

Because the technology behind Internet marketing has gotten so darn exact, we can scale our marketing efforts like never before. Strategically applied, marketing automation allows us to prove exactly how our campaigns affect revenue. What's to hate about that?

1. http://www.slideshare.net/PepperGlobal/pepper-global-2014-marketing-automation-report
2. http://blogs.position2.com/infographic-digital-marketing-trends-predictions-2014
3. http://blog.hubspot.com/blog/tabid/6307/bid/28943/25-Jaw-Dropping-Marketing-Automa-tion-Stats-Data.aspx
4. http://blogs.position2.com/infographic-digital-marketing-trends-predictions-2014
5. http://www.marketo.com/marketing-automation/

You want to have butterflies in your Stomach, because if you don't, if you walk out on stage Complacent, that's not a Good thing.

— Joan Jett

CHAPTER 34

The Future of Content and Social

Where Marketing is Going... in 2015 and Beyond

2015 is going to be an epic year for marketers and writers. It's the year that content, social, search, and email are coming together, working in sync for the greater good of marketing-kind. It's also the year that wise marketing departments will use analytics and automation to scale their efforts and make better decisions. It's the year that content will tip from being an interesting option to being a must-have.

And paired with that, it's the year of the writer—in other words, the year that content creators begin to be valued as the creators of valuable *assets*, rather than an expense on the balance sheet. It's the future of marketing and it's sitting at our doorstep. But as is so often the case, to understand the future, we must look to the past.

In the beginning, there was Lead Generation

Picture the B2B marketer at the beginning of the twenty-first century deciding to embrace the new science of demand generation, announcing to their sales team, "Let there be leads." Lead generation was becoming like Ron Burgundy (kind of a big deal). But lead generation, or lead gen, was in its very early stages. Marketing teams would send out tons of direct mail as part of massive campaigns, and prospects would literally tear off a business reply card and mail it back. Or marketers would collect business cards at trade shows.

Now they had a "lead" to hand over to sales, but this was a very tedious process. Fast-forward a few years as email marketing began to make waves. At first, mostly B2C companies benefitted. B2B marketers would begin to make the transition from direct mail to email, but it was still a new strategy and they were slow to catch on. Powered by vendors like GotMarketing, ExactTarget, Boomerang, and VerticalResponse, each month marketers would go back to their database with a new offer, essentially taking a spray-and-pray approach to "engagement." Every person who responded got a call regardless of their interest level.

During this time, a lead was a lead. Neither sales nor marketing could figure out if the lead was hot, warm, or cold. Deciding which leads to call became a very painful process and a source of tension for both marketing and sales teams. The concept of prioritizing leads would become a very hot topic, but no one had the technology to do anything about it.

All leads are not created equal

There was clearly a need for something new. Early marketing tools from Genius and Marketbright started to make some headway with website tracking technology. But it wasn't enough. Marketers needed a platform that would tie everything together. Enter marketing automation, a godsend for B2B marketers looking for one central platform for all of their campaigns.

No longer did marketers have to manually comb through the massive number of raw inquiries; now they had software to do this in addition to so much more. Marketing automation would empower them to build and manage multiple campaigns from start to finish while automating many of the mundane tasks associated with lead management. In this new era, marketers could create landing pages, score and nurture leads, and effectively measure the ROI of their marketing efforts—all on one platform.

In addition, they could now track the digital body language of their prospects and determine who's hot and who's not. This would prove increasingly important as the seller-controlled buying process would soon give way to the empowered-buyer process. Today's buyers do much of their own research, not wanting or needing to engage with sales until they're nearly through the entire buying process. This change has forced marketing departments to take a bigger role in developing and nurturing the prospect relationship.

Along with marketing automation came a new, smarter kind of marketing. The other side of the automation coin is a new, more effective style of marketing that supports and improves the sales process. Smart content marketing helps sales teams by answering objections, showcasing customer success, demonstrating benefits, and even uncovering prospect pain points. Effective advertising has always been "salesmanship in print." Content—which has actually been used in good advertising for more than 100 years—just does a better job of it.

Along with the rise of content, we're seeing the rise of the content creator—the capable writer, video producer, or podcast publisher who can make the content that prospects want to consume. Wise businesses know that talent doesn't come cheap, but that high-quality content is an investment that tends to pay off handsomely.

New content marketing platforms are emerging as an important tool for content creators. These new solutions, integrated with marketing and sales automation, empower them to quickly learn what content works and doesn't work for greater content impact.

Where we're going, we don't need roads

Over a century ago, the department-store magnate John Wanamaker famously said, "I know half my advertising dollars are wasted. I just don't know which half." Fast-forward to 2014—this is no longer an issue.

Modern marketers have more data available at their fingertips than ever before. And marketing automation allows them to convert that data into actionable insights. No longer is there any question around the return on their marketing spend and how that spend contributes to driving revenue; there are now hard metrics to report.

As marketing automation begins moving into the mainstream and is quickly becoming the hot topic at marketing conferences around the world, it promises to transform the marketer's role. The analytics that this technology provides will prove and improve marketing spend and finally give the marketer a seat at the revenue table.

CHAPTER 35

It's a Long Way to the Top if You Want to Rock 'n' Roll

Now I would like to turn the focus on you, the marketer who is ready to make a difference and lead instead of follow. If there are two things that I've learned matter most during my own journey, it's your network and your personal brand. It takes time and dedication to build both of these successfully and you get out of it only what you put in.

Here are my personal recommendations for every marketer who reads this book in regards to next steps.

1. Claim your online identity, it's the foundation for building your personal brand—It's just not okay to let your LinkedIn profile collect Internet dust until you're actively looking for your next job.

If your profile isn't current, or if it communicates indifference, not only are you likely missing career-transforming opportunities, but you could also be giving people the wrong impression. Start with the basics. Put down a solid foundation and add to it over time. How, you ask? Like this:

- Make sure work experience and résumé data are up to date.

- Post a picture that doesn't include a beer (unless you're a brewer).

- Add rich media to your profile. (This is the one online place where it's OK to brag about yourself a little bit.)

- Reach out to trusted peers for recommendations.

- Join and participate in relevant groups.

2. Write every single day—This is the cornerstone of any good content creator. The ability to tell stories, write complete sentences, and drum up compelling content takes practice. So practice. Identify a topic, and work on developing different story angles and new ways to say the same thing. Unlock your creative genius by picking up a pen, or by stomping your fingers on your computer. Do it, and do it every day.

3. Find the folks who can make you successful and build strong relationships with them—Identify the folks in your organization that will be critical to your success and befriend them. Building strong relationships early on will help you moving forward and very likely result in them wanting to help you as well. I recommend reading "The First 90 Days" each and every time you start a new gig or new position. And don't forget the global folks; don't just jump on a conference call with them. Use video and get as much face-to-face time with them. Even though they are overseas, technology can allow you to build a solid relationship with them just as if they are in the office next door.

4. Share and engage every single day—Take 20 minutes a day to read, share, and engage with your social networks. Adding your two cents by commenting, sharing, and tagging folks is an incredibly powerful way to get on people's radars, but you have to be consistent. Build a list of influencers who matter to you,

and amplify their content with your own spin, and do it often. Ask not what your influencers can do for you; ask what you can do for your influencers. In time, they will very likely reciprocate.

5. Create a Content "Sizzle Reel"—In the world of "everyone's a content creator," there's no excuse for not having something to showcase. Be it a personal blog, a fun SlideShare presentation, or an engaging Flickr profile, some sort of example is necessary. If you have previous experience, go through the metrics of your best work, review the impact and analytics, and put together a portfolio. This is your highlight reel, which shows you can make an impact and that you understand what makes content successful. Was your infographic featured on an important blog? Did your newsjacking make any real headlines? Did a thought leader share a piece of your content? How many opportunities did you generate? Include what matters.

6. Put together an action plan—Put together a simple 30-60-90 day plan for success. What do you ultimately want to achieve? Is it a face-to-face meeting with an influencer? The opportunity to guest blog on your favorite marketing site? To publish once a week on LinkedIn? Start simple and celebrate each win. This stuff takes time, but the sooner you start, the sooner you will see an impact.

Thanks for reading this book and feel free to connect with me on LinkedIn[1] and share any feedback or comments. As Ozzy Osbourne would say, "Goodnight, I love you all."

Now go create some bloody good content!

Jason

---

1. https://www.linkedin.com/in/jsnmiller

SIDE 4: APPENDIX AND SPECIAL THANKS

17 Essential Blogs You Should Be Reading Daily

One thing I am frequently asked is what blogs I subscribe to and read on a daily basis to keep up on news, trends, and all things marketing. Here are the ones that I read every single day so that I never miss a beat. I use Pulse[1] as my reader and have a custom channel dedicated to these remarkable blogs. The blogs listed below are my personal favorites. If there is such a thing as a PhD in online marketing, this is where they would pull the classroom materials from, so take full advantage of this cornucopia of free knowledge for marketers.

1. http://moz.com/blog
    For all things SEO and beyond, Whiteboard Fridays are a MUST watch. Rand Fishkin is a genius.

2. http://www.copyblogger.com/blog/
    The smartest folks in the world on how to tie everything together; SEO, Social, Content, and more. Brilliant stuff.

3. http://www.annhandley.com/
    Chief Content Officer at MarketingProfs and author of Everybody Writes, Ann is the queen of content marketing and storytelling for business.

4. http://contentmarketinginstitute.com/blog/
    It's an institute dedicated to content marketing founded by the Godfather of content Mr. Joe Pulizzi. Enough said.

5. http://www.toprankblog.com/
    A little bit of everything; a whole lotta' awesome.

6. http://www.convinceandconvert.com/blog/
    Daily goodness from Jay Baer and company.

7. http://www.briansolis.com/
   Insights from one of the most forward-thinking marketers on the planet.

8. http://sethgodin.typepad.com/
   The man, the legend, essential daily reading for all marketers.

9. http://www.socialmediaexaminer.com/
   A full lesson in social media marketing every single day.

10. https://www.marketingtechblog.com/
    Bleeding-edge marketing from Doug Karr and company.

11. http://www.funnelholic.com/
    Craig Rosenberg might actually be the real "most interesting man in the world." Fantastic insights around the intersection of all things content marketing, social media, and sales and marketing.

12. http://chrisbrogan.com/blog/
    Incredibly inspiring posts on marketing and most recently Brogan's remarkable journey to becoming both mentally and physically fit. Real world marketing advice from a guy who tells it like it is.

13. http://www.internetmarketingninjas.com/blog/
    This is one of those hidden gem blogs that is super helpful around SEO, content and social media. Ann Smarty is one of the contributors and she is brilliant.

14. http://www.b2bmarketinginsider.com/
    Newscred's VP of Content Michael Brenner delivers fantastic B2B marketing content each and every week.

15. http://www.heinzmarketing.com/matt-on-marketing/blog/
    Matt is the master of aligning sales and marketing and shares tips, tricks, strategies and tactics for doing so efficiently.

16. http://heidicohen.com/
    Heidi's posts are incredibly detailed. It's sort of like getting a full marketing lesson in a condensed format for the very busy marketer. Fantastic insights from a super smart marketer.

17. http://www.curata.com/blog/
Curata's CEO, Pawan Deshpande, and CMO, Michael Gerard, know what it takes to develop and execute a content marketing strategy; and they share their tactics, tips and templates every week to help make content marketers more successful."

(My version of album liner notes)

Special thanks to all the marketers who shaped this book in one way or another and inspire me to be a better marketer: Brian Clark, Tony Clark, Ann Handley, Joe Pulizzi, Maria Pergolino, Michael Brenner, Jon Miller, Peter Lobi, Nick Cicero, Jason Keath, Amber Naslund, Laura Fitton, Joe Chernov, Craig Rosenberg, Justin Gray, Matt Heinz, Deanna Lazzaroni, Keith Richey, Koka Sexton, Dennis Yu, Chris Buehler, Scorch Agency, Stephanie Tilton, Michael Stelzner, C.C. Chapman, Chris Brogan, Todd Wheatland, Lee Odden, Neal Schaffer, Ekaterina Walter, Aaron Kahlow, Barry Feldman, Stephanie Losee, Rebecca Lieb, Jeremiah Owyang, Brian Solis, Dennis Goedegebuure, Jascha Kaykas-wolff, Jesse Noyes, Seth Godin, Heidi Cohen, Carmen Hill, Tim Hayden, Connie Benson, Pawan Deshpande, Michael Gerard, and anyone I forgot to mention who I've met over the years.

1. https://www.pulse.me/

Sources

1. http://contentmarketinginstitute.com/what-is-content-marketing/

2. http://marketingland.com/social-media-driving-revenue-for-one-third-of-b2c-companies-one-fifth-of-b2b-firms-report-64256

3. http://www.emarketer.com/Article/How-B2Bs-Working-Social-Leads/1010162#sthash.Q4Z82DGp.dpuf

4. http://www.slideshare.net/hootsuite/case-studymarketo-32413372

5. https://www.linkedin.com/ads/

6. http://www.copyblogger.com/native-advertising-2014/

7. http://www.iab.net/media/file/Sharethrough-IPG-Infographic-11x17-CMYK_nobleeds.pdf

8. http://www.woodst.com/content-marketing/5-questions-with-joe-pulizzi-founder-of-content-marketing-institute/

9. http://www.cmocouncil.org/

10. http://www.slideshare.net/marketo/marketing-secret-sauce-scottsdale-june-2014

11. https://www.google.com/webhp?sourceid=chrome-instant&ion=1&espv=2&ie=UTF-8#q=Definition%20of%20an%20infographic

12. http://localization.cloudwords.com/GlobalMarketingReport.html

13. http://blog.marketo.com/2013/02/what-is-the-difference-between-thought-leadership-and-content-marketing.html

14. http://www.slideshare.net/SAVO_Group/techniques-of-social-selling-just-do-it-sales-for-life

15. http://www.inpwrd.com/nielsen

16. http://mashable.com/2012/06/21/bird-poop-smartcar/

17. http://www.aberdeen.com/research/8138/ip-social-media-selling/content.aspx

18. http://www.internetmarketingninjas.com/blog/content/free-keyword-research-tools-search-suggestions/

Made in the USA
Middletown, DE
28 August 2015